Elements in Eighteenth-Century Connections
edited by
Eve Tavor Bannet
University of Oklahoma
Markman Ellis
Queen Mary University of London

THE ART OF THE ACTRESS

Fashioning Identities

Laura Engel
Duquesne University

Shaftesbury Road, Cambridge CB2 8EA, United Kingdom

One Liberty Plaza, 20th Floor, New York, NY 10006, USA

477 Williamstown Road, Port Melbourne, VIC 3207, Australia

314–321, 3rd Floor, Plot 3, Splendor Forum, Jasola District Centre,
New Delhi – 110025, India

103 Penang Road, #05–06/07, Visioncrest Commercial, Singapore 238467

Cambridge University Press is part of Cambridge University Press & Assessment,
a department of the University of Cambridge.

We share the University's mission to contribute to society through the pursuit of
education, learning and research at the highest international levels of excellence.

www.cambridge.org
Information on this title: www.cambridge.org/9781009486811

DOI: 10.1017/9781108973519

First published 2024

A catalogue record for this publication is available from the British Library

ISBN 978-1-009-48681-1 Hardback
ISBN 978-1-108-97790-6 Paperback
ISSN 2632-5578 (online)
ISSN 2632-556X (print)

The Art of the Actress

Fashioning Identities

Elements in Eighteenth-Century Connections

DOI: 10.1017/9781108973519
First published online: January 2024

Laura Engel
Duquesne University

Author for correspondence: Laura Engel, engell784@duq.edu

Abstract: This Element looks at the art of the actress in the eighteenth century. It considers how visual materials across genres, such as prints, portraits, sculpture, costumes, and accessories, contribute to the understanding of the nuances of female celebrity, fame, notoriety, and scandal. The 'art' of the actress refers to the actress represented in visual art, as well as to the actress's labor and skill in making art ephemerally through performance and tangibly through objects. Moving away from the concept of the 'actress as muse,' a relationship that privileges the role of the male artist over the inspirational subject, the author focuses instead on the varied significance of representations, reproductions, and re-animations of actresses, female artists, and theatrical women across media. Via case studies, the Element explores how the archive charts both a familiar and at times unknown narrative about female performers of the past.

Keywords: actresses, eighteenth century, female artists, portraits, fashion

ISBNs: 9781009486811 (HB), 9781108977906 (PB), 9781108973519 (OC)
ISSNs: 2632-5578 (online), 2632-556X (print)

Contents

Introduction: The Art of the Actress in the Eighteenth Century

> Hold, are you mad? You damn'd confounded dog!
> I am to rise and speak the epilogue.
> I come, kind gentlemen, strange news to tell ye;
> I am the ghost of poor departed Nelly.
> Sweet ladies be not frightened; I'll be civil,
> I'm what I was, a little harmless devil.
> For after death, we sprites have just such natures
> We had for all the world, when human creatures;
> And therefore, I that was an actress here,
> Play all my tricks in Hell, a goblin there.
> Gallants, look to't you say there are no sprites;
> But I'll come dance about your beds at nights.
> And faith you'll be in a sweet kind of taking,
> When I surprise you between sleep and waking.
> To tell you true, I walk because I die
> Out of my calling in a tragedy. . . .
> As for my epitaph when I am gone,
> I'll trust no poet, but will write my own.
> Here Nelly lies, who, though she liv'd a slattern,
> Yet died a princess, acting in Saint Catherine.[1]

John Dryden's epilogue for *Tyrannick Love* (1669), written specifically for the Restoration actress and famed mistress to Charles II, Nell Gwyn, provides us with a sense of what her talents may have been as a performer. She begins by rising from the dead, drawing attention to the ontology of performance and the meta-theatrics of the stage. Nell Gwyn exists on two planes simultaneously – she is both the role that she portrays onstage and herself as a living embodied presence. Her assertion challenges the audience's sense of illusion and breaks the fourth wall. Even more compelling is the idea that she emerges as "the ghost of poor departed Nelly," a liminal figure who occupies the space between both embodied states. This deliberate ephemerality gives her the power to haunt people. Onstage she is an "actress," but as a sprite in Hell she is a "goblin." As a "sprite" she assures the ladies that she will be "civil," for "I'm what I was, a little harmless devil." Making light of her seductive charms and tendency toward mischief for the women in the audience, she then addresses the "gallants" with the promise that she will "surprise" them "between waking and sleeping." The actress's art is something that performs on people both during the play and afterward, lingering in ways that can be sexual and unsettling.

---

[1] Dryden, *Tyrannick Love*, n.p.

As Joseph Roach has eloquently argued, through the writings of Samuel Pepys we can trace the idea of the pervasive afterimage of early actresses as a way of conceptualizing the history of female celebrity and allure. Gwyn occupies a prominent space in this trajectory.[2] Dryden clearly recognized this kind of aftereffect when he wrote this epilogue for Gwyn to perform. What we do not have here, however, is the powerful embodied presence of Gwyn herself. In performance, this speech must have contained and signaled a variety of other kinds of meanings for the audience. When Gwyn declares, "To tell you true, I walk because I die / Out of my calling in a tragedy," there would likely be a pun detected in the word "die," also a synonym for orgasm, but in another sense Gwyn herself is asserting that she has life because of her job as an actress. It is her art (her creative process, labor, and ingenuity) that defines and sustains her existence. For a woman who could not read and only learned to write later in her life, Gwyn's announcement at the end of the epilogue that she will craft her own "epitaph" is mediated through her strategic embodied performances – onstage and in her own life. The joke that she started as a prostitute and ended up onstage acting as a princess is an assertion of agency in performance and a prophetic mapping of her future.

This Element looks at the art of the actress in the eighteenth century. I consider how visual materials across genres, such as prints, portraits, sculpture, costume, and accessories, contribute to our understanding of the nuances of female celebrity, fame, notoriety, and scandal. The "art" of the actress thus refers to the actress represented in art, as well as to the actress's labor and skill in making art ephemerally through performance and tangibly through objects. Moving away from the concept of the "actress as muse," a relationship that privileges the role of the male artist over the inspirational subject, I focus instead on the varied significance of representations, reproductions, and reanimations of actresses, female artists, and theatrical women across media. Through specific case studies, I explore how the archive charts both a familiar and at times unknown narrative about female performers of the past.

Actresses' images were everywhere in the long eighteenth century; they appeared throughout visual media in portraits, miniatures, prints, caricatures, periodical illustrations, sculpture, and porcelain. The proliferation of materials representing actresses in various formats signaled the public's interest in women on the stage and in celebrity culture in general. For female celebrities in particular, the blurred distinction between actresses *and* artworks, and actresses *as* artworks, foregrounds a central paradox for women onstage that

---

[2] See Roach's discussion of Gwyn and the afterlife of celebrity in *It*, pp. 63–6. See also McGirr, "Nell Gwyn's Breasts and Colley Cibber's Shirts," pp. 13–34.

persists – that is, the ways in which the visibility of the female figure and the cultural politics of female embodiment often mask the professionalism, labor, and skill of female performers. Actresses' visual presences across various genres and formats can potentially provide traces of their lost "art." I am not arguing that there is a one-to-one correspondence between what actresses did onstage and how they were portrayed in print, but I do want to suggest that there are potentially important links between the embodied actions of actresses and subsequent representations of them. In certain cases, with more famous actresses, we can glean a sense of their rippling aftereffects through reading multiple images of them across materials.

Much of the scholarship about eighteenth-century actresses and female artists in the public sphere has centered on famous figures simply because there is more material about them.[3] This Element is meant to be read as a visual exhibition highlighting the representations, creative works, collaborations, and experiences of both well-established and lesser-known performers. The sections are organized thematically as case studies. I analyze pearls as paradoxical accessories for actresses, female aristocrats, and Restoration women artists; the actress as artist and the artist as actress using the works of Angelica Kauffman and Anne Damer; and actresses and satire highlighting the scandalous mistress Mary Anne Clarke and her muff. I finally offer an epilogue on Thomas Lawrence's unfinished portraits of Elizabeth Inchbald and Lady Emilia Cahir, exploring the aftermath of the art of the actress. Each section considers specific figures and the resonance of their art (visual and theatrical) across a variety of materials.

Eighteenth-century actresses were at the center of the materialization of conflicting ideologies about female performance and embodiment. From the arrival of actresses on the stage in 1660 to the end of the eighteenth century, when certain actresses had established themselves as legitimate superstars, the figure of the actress becomes a kind of interdisciplinary heroine able to cross genres and epitomize a new kind of agency and/or identity category for women.[4] The significance of the actress is also tied to emerging academic conversations about amateur and professional women artists, writers, and performers. The art of the actress can tell us important things about how women fashioned their identities on- and offstage, as well as how audiences

---

[3] For more about mid-to-late eighteenth-century actresses and portraiture, see West, *Image of the Actor*; Asleson, ed., *Passion for Performance, Notorious Muse*; Perry, *Spectacular Flirtations*; Engel, *Fashioning Celebrity*; Nussbaum, *Rival Queens*; McPherson, *Art and Celebrity*. For works on early actresses, see MacLeod and Marciari Alexander, eds., *Painted Ladies*; Perry, Roach, and West, eds., *First Actresses*. For an overview of actress studies and books about eighteenth-century actresses and celebrity, see Engel, "Stage Beauties."

[4] See Nussbaum, *Rival Queens*.

perceived women in the public sphere through theatrical lenses. I am using the terms "actress" and "performance" somewhat broadly here. Although there is certainly a difference between actresses who are paid to be onstage and women who perform theatrically offstage, modes of female performance and the scripts of female performativity exist both on- and offstage with the same kinds of visual cues and identity markers. Portraits are a heightened form of idealized reality, as are satiric prints. The repeated appearance of particular visual markers – accessories, poses, costumes, and hairstyles – suggests an eighteenth-century audience trained to recognize visual cues connected to female performers and to messages about them. The availability of images of famous actresses (for example, Dorothy Jordan) creates a powerful mechanism for analogy or comparison to lesser-known public figures such as Mary Anne Clarke. At the same time, female artists choosing to represent themselves in ways that echo depictions of female performers offer ways to think about the theatricality necessary for women artists to fashion their public and professional identities. In addition, considering the centrality of fashion – specifically accessories such as pearls and muffs as potent signifiers attached to a variety of women, and easily read by audiences in a range of ways – gives us some access to the layered and often conflicting messages surrounding actresses and the danger and possibilities of their allure.

Focusing on the art of the actress from the actress's perspective offers possibilities for highlighting actresses' agency in shaping their personas, as well as the limitations of their self-fashioning strategies. It is important to consider the differences and connections between an actress sitting for her portrait, an artist modeling herself alongside actresses or as an actress, an artist using an image of a female performer multiple times in her work, actresses making their own self-portraits, and artists trying to capture the ephemerality of actresses' performances in their work. Each of these modalities represents another way to approach the art of the actress beyond the traditional formulation of a male painter capturing a likeness of an actress/muse. Shifting the emphasis onto the art of the actress turns our attention toward the significance of female friendships, networks, and collaborations.

The arrival of the actresses in the eighteenth century is central to understanding unfolding anxieties about the nation, race, gender, and heteronormativity. Ideologies of race and empire, particularly in relation to early actresses as new commodities in a world with foreign queens and mistresses, eventually led to an alignment of well-known actresses with the virtues of British nationalism.[5]

---

[5] For more on the connections among Restoration actresses, foreign queens, and empire, see L. Rosenthal, *Ways of the World*.

Sarah Siddons's role as Britannia (onstage and in portraits) solidified actresses' ambiguous connection to whiteness and Englishness by the end of the century. Yet, by looking closely at the resonance of female performers and their public theatrics and art, an alternative narrative of resistance emerges. Nell Gwyn's self-fashioning through expensive accessories, Angelica Kauffman's celebration of other female performers alongside her own self-representations, Anne Damer's artistic collaborations with female artists and performers, Mary Anne Clarke's brave and theatrical attempt to overthrow her lover the Duke of York, and Elizabeth Inchbald's creation of haunting and memorable roles for actresses (stemming in part from her own experience as an actress) provide new ways of looking at the impact and resonance of female performers and their performances.

Sections

Section 1, "The Paradox of Pearls," explores the complex ways in which pearls appear in portraits of celebrated and imagined figures in the early eighteenth century. The ubiquity of pearls in these images highlights the simultaneous rise and threat of female visibility and performance in the court of Charles II. Pearls in pictures of Restoration women evoke connections between the emergence of actresses as exotic, dazzling commodities and the pervasive and dangerous effects of empire. Turning at the end of the section to the female artists Joan Carlile, Mary Beale, and Anne Killigrew, I examine how their use of pearls in self-portraits helped fashion their images as both creative professionals and beautiful theatrical subjects, aligning their visual identities with aristocrats and actresses.

Section 2, "The Actress As Artist and the Artist As Actress," considers the connections between the work of the artist Angelica Kauffman and the sculptress, actress, and novelist Anne Damer. For Kauffman and Damer, the inextricable relationship between artistic practice and performance is evident in the ways in which they represent themselves. Kauffman's many self-portraits dramatize the relationship between the act of being an artist and the multifaceted meanings of appearing as oneself. A series of portraits of theatrical women that Kauffman completed in the 1790s echoes one of her most famous self-portraits now in the Uffizi Gallery and displayed in the same room as Anne Damer's marble bust of herself. Damer's aesthetic, drawn from antique sculpture, emphasized the idealized beauty and serenity of her female subjects. In contrast to the elegant pathos and solemnity of her portrait busts, Damer's performances in private theatricals were characterized by her dazzling costumes and ornate accessories. The tension between Damer's art forms – the permanence of sculpture and the ephemerality of performance – is similar to the pull that Kauffman dramatizes in her self-portraits between the artistic practices of painting and singing. Damer's and Kauffman's ties to "the art of the actress" evoke a history of female collaborations and artistic networks.

Section 3, "Mary Anne's Muff: Actresses and Satire," uses an extended case study of satiric prints of Mary Anne Clarke, courtesan, actress, and mistress, to explore the relationship between actresses, politics, seduction, and caricature. In 1809 Mary Anne Clarke, the mistress of the Duke of York (the king's second son and commander in chief of the armed forces), testified before Parliament that she had sold army commissions to the highest bidders to decorate the large mansion bequeathed to her by her royal lover. Mary Anne Clarke's theatricality and fashion choices, particularly the large white muff she wore to testify at the House of Commons, feature prominently in many satiric prints by well-known caricaturists such as Thomas Rowlandson. Clarke's attempts to represent herself as an innocent heroine are parodied through references to her role as a mistress, her desire for fame and luxury, and her connections to famous actresses such as Sarah Siddons and Dorothy Jordan (the latter herself the longtime mistress of the Duke of Clarence).

In a brief epilogue, "Unfinished Business: Elizabeth Inchbald, Lady Cahir, Sir Thomas Lawrence, and the Aftermath of the Art of the Actress," I consider two unfinished portraits by Sir Thomas Lawrence of the actress, playwright, and novelist Elizabeth Inchbald and the Irish aristocrat and amateur actress Lady Emilia Cahir. The painting of Lady Cahir, inspired by her performance in Elizabeth Inchbald's play *The Wedding Day*, in which she acted opposite Lawrence in the Bentley Priory Private Theatricals, is a startling example of the aftereffects of the art of the actress. The haunting and lasting impression Inchbald and Lady Cahir both made on Thomas Lawrence connects us as contemporary spectators to the process of their artistic production and to the resonant impacts of their performances.

1 The Paradox of Pearls

Pearls figure prominently in pictures of celebrated women across the eighteenth century. From the first superstar actress and mistress to King Charles II, Nell Gwyn (Figure 1), to the most famous female celebrity of the late eighteenth century, Sarah Siddons, the mysterious, opaque, and gleaming white accessory aligns with the equally mutable, seductive, and threatening role of the actress. Worn around the neck as a choker, a collar, or in ropes or strands; in hair woven through tendrils; as earrings; draped around the body and bodice as a decorative

Figure 1 *Nell Gwyn* by Simon Verelst, ca. 1680. National Portrait Gallery

element; or embedded in the settings of jewels, boxes, frames, miniatures, and brooches – pearls adorn, trespass, and transgress. They accessorize and colonize. They highlight and fetishize. They perform.[6]

In this section, I connect the intangible performances of pearls, their multiple meanings, and variable value to the art of the actress both on- and offstage. Elsewhere, I have written about the links between portraits and the dynamics of performance.[7] Drawing on Rebecca Schneider's concept of "performing remains," I contend that portraits contain the traces of past encounters, relationships, and desires that are reignited when people look at them – both in the past and in the present.[8] The performative dynamics of portraits are translated to viewers in specific ways through visual codes. Clothing, accessories, and jewelry perform as part of a complex series of messages. Tracing representations of pearls in portraits of Restoration actresses, artists, and aristocrats broadens our sense of the ways in which women were seen, as well as the ways in which they wished to represent themselves. As an expensive, elegant accessory, pearls appear in portraits of actresses to signify the often ambiguous "value" of their performances, particularly in relation to their introduction to the

---

[6] For more on the history, distribution, marketing, and cultural meaning of pearls, see Warsh, *American Baroque*; Shen, *Pearls*; Joyce and Addison, *Pearls*. For discussions of pearls in eighteenth-century portraits and fashion, see Pointon, *Brilliant Effects*; Ribeiro, *Dress and Morality*.

[7] Engel, *Women, Performance, and the Material of Memory*, pp. 57–60.

[8] See Schneider, *Performing Remains*.

theater as brilliant new commodities in 1660. Pearls in portraits of Restoration women offer connections between the novelty, sexuality, and agency of early actresses and the seductive and insidious power of empire. Turning to female artists and their use of pearls in self-portraits later in this section, I suggest that we can learn something important about how women wished to represent themselves as creative professionals and beautiful subjects.

1.1 Women, Pearls, and Visual Legacies

As one of the most sought-after commodities of the early modern colonial enterprise, precious jewels tied to bondage, slavery, and violence, pearls have a baroque and complex history. The historian Molly A. Warsh argues that pearls represented a particular kind of paradox for female subjects in the late seventeenth century: "In the context of rising debates about luxury and consumption and concern about the increased visibility and political prominence of women in the aftermath of the tumult of the English Civil War and Protectorate, pearls' natural, reflective beauty could absorb the dueling fantasies of women as controllable and uncontrolled" (Figure 2).[9] Moreover, in her majestic study of

Figure 2 *Anne Hyde, Duchess of York*, after Sir Peter Lely, oil on canvas, feigned oval, based on a work of circa 1668–70. National Portrait Gallery

---

[9] Warsh, *American Baroque*, p. 221.

early modern jewelry, Marcia Pointon argues that pearls always suggest a duality between life and death.[10] Further, according to Warsh, "by the end of the seventeenth century, pearls were linked in the popular imagination to women's political identity and to their perceived virtue and worth."[11] In the same way that the presence of pearls signaled the simultaneous rise and threat of female agency and visibility at the court of Charles II, representations of pearls in portraits of actresses channeled the ambiguity surrounding their power, prestige, and precarious social standing. Actresses posed a specific challenge to established modes of female identity and containment. They were not legitimate members of the aristocracy, yet some became an integral part of the court through their strategic liaisons. Pointon explains that pearls signified chastity and sexuality simultaneously: "They are an attribute of chastity in representations of the Virgin Mary (for example in Hans Memling's Madonna of 1487 in Bruges and in Tintoretto's *Tarquin and Lucretia* in the Chicago Art Institute), but they were also worn by the whore of Babylon in the Apocalypse."[12] Portraits of actresses with pearls thus reflect the tenuous nature of their position in society and the very real anxieties circulating about their disruptive power.

A century before the restoration of Charles II, portraits of Queen Elizabeth I in ropes of pearls established her figure as emblematic of the body politic and the British Empire.[13] In the mid-eighteenth century the author, architect, and collector Horace Walpole highlighted pearls as a distinctive feature of Queen Elizabeth I's visual legacy: "A pale Roman nose, a head of hair loaded with crowns and powdered with diamonds, a vast ruff, a vaster fardingale, and a bushel of pearls are features by which everybody knows at once the pictures of Queen Elizabeth" (Figure 3).[14] Even in death, Elizabeth's wax figure was adorned in "spherical pearls in wax, long necklaces of them, a great pearl-ornamented stomacher, pearl earrings with large pear-shaped pedants, and even broad pearl medallions on the shoebows."[15] Depictions of Elizabeth's pearls as symbols of her extraordinary wealth and the range of her empire are also inextricably linked to the fake wax accessories that decorate

---

[10] Pointon, *Brilliant Effects*, p. 108.   [11] Warsh, *American Baroque*, p. 220.

[12] Pointon, *Brilliant Effects*, p. 116. The ambiguity of pearls is also present in Pointon's discussion of Sir Joshua Reynolds's portrait of the courtesan Kitty Fisher as Cleopatra: "This courtesan is posing as a queen familiar in history and fable but, for an eighteenth-century audience, Kitty stood for the ephemeral, for an identity that could not be anchored, for a chameleon-like female independence all the more dangerous for being centred in the visible space of a masculine desire to possess" (p. 123).

[13] On the visual legacies of Queen Elizabeth I, see Sharpe, "Thy Longing Country's Darling," p. 10; Doran, ed., *Elizabeth and Mary*.

[14] Walpole, *Anecdotes of Painting in England*, p. 84.

[15] Kunz and Stevenson, *Book of the Pearl*, p. 454.

Figure 3 *Queen Elizabeth I (The Ditchley Portrait)*, by Marcus Geeraerts the Younger, 1592. National Portrait Gallery

her coffin. It is difficult to assess the value of a pearl unless you are holding it in your hand and looking at it closely.[16] This tension between authenticity and illusion is central to the allure of pearls and to the art of the actress (the legacy of Queen Mary I of England and the Peregrine Pearl, which eventually was owned by the actress Elizabeth Taylor, also contributes to the series of connections among pearls, royalty, and actresses). Actresses' ability to mimic and disguise themselves allowed them to blur the boundaries between their roles onstage and their performances offstage. The availability of pearls, both expensive and affordable, increased in the seventeenth century, at the same moment when the performance, sexuality, and power of women in and around the court of Charles II were being celebrated in images of them wearing a wide array of pearl accessories.

---

[16] Shen, *Pearls*, pp. 30–48.

Figure 4 *Henrietta Maria*, after Sir Anthony Van Dyck, oil on canvas, seventeenth century, based on a work of circa 1632–5. National Portrait Gallery

1.2 Queens, Ladies, Mistresses, and Pearls

Early seventeenth-century court painters, such as Anthony Van Dyck (1599–1641), portrayed a variety of women wearing pearls. In his 1636 portrait of Queen Henrietta Maria (Figure 4), the queen looks thoughtfully out at the viewer, her hands clasped deliberately over her rounding pregnant belly. She wears a strand of pearls around her neck, and the bodice of her dress is adorned with pearl trimming that runs around her breast, joining in a loop that draws the eye down toward her unborn progeny. Pearls in this image signify wealth, production, and Henrietta's role as a queen in furthering the line of a nation. Van Dyck's painting of his mistress Margaret Lemon (ca. 1638), also wearing a single strand of pearls, is a more intimate view of the subject. Margaret is seen in profile looking over her shoulder at the viewer. She holds a piece of drapery around her shoulders, which may or may not be all that she is wearing. Pearls in this image suggest sexuality, sensuality, and availability. In the portrait of his wife, Mary Lady Van Dyck, circa 1640 (Figure 5), Lady Van Dyck is presented as a fashionable, confident woman, portraying through her beauty the dynamic skills of her artist husband. She wears a pearl necklace with pendant earrings and a decorative oak accessory in her hair. Her gown is made of expensive,

Figure 5 *Mary (née Ruthven), Lady Van Dyck,* by Richard Gaywood, after Sir Anthony Van Dyck, published by Peter Stent, etching, mid-seventeenth century. National Portrait Gallery

luxurious fabric and she holds a beaded crucifix in her hands, a symbol of her Catholicism and fidelity. Pearls represent a combination of signifiers here – wealth, status, fashion, Catholicism, fidelity, fertility (Mary would give birth to a daughter in 1641).

The court painter Peter Lely (1618–80) would borrow from Van Dyck's use of pearls in his images of actresses, mistresses, and aristocrats of the court of Charles II, particularly in his series known as the "Windsor Beauties." According to Catherine MacLeod and Julia Marciari Alexander, "These paintings, which hang in the Communications Gallery at Hampton Court Palace today, apparently formed the heart of Lely's work for his important royal patrons, the Duke and Duchess of York, in the years just following the Restoration." MacLeod and Marciari Alexander go on to observe, "Beautiful, decorative, fashionable, and hung harmoniously together, the portraits of these women must have provoked comment, admiration and awe, gossip and nudges, and even, perhaps, smirks and giggles from their audiences.

Such portraits would have marked their owners as court insiders, among those most 'in the know.'"[17] Pearls form a connective thread that links these images together. In all eleven portraits, the sitters are wearing some form of pearls, as necklaces, earrings, decorative motifs, clasps, brooches, and hair ornaments. Some women appear as themselves and others appear as goddesses or saints (for example, Barbara Villiers as Minerva,[18] Elizabeth Hamilton as Saint Catherine). Pearls anchor these figures as present in the moment of time and context that produced them as specific types of celebrities famous for their allure, wealth, position, and sensuality.

1.3 Nell Gwyn and Margaret Hughes: Actress Beauties

Portraits of the actresses and well-known mistresses Nell Gwyn and Margaret Hughes wearing pearls echo the Windsor Beauties series along with a range of portraits of Restoration women that fall into three often-overlapping categories – portraits that highlight pearls as fashionable accessories representing wealth and luxury; pictures that conflate pearls with mythology and sexuality; and images that underscore pearls as signifiers of whiteness, empire, and power. Gwyn's and Hughes's association with other powerful women at court through a visual legacy of pearls underscores the blurred boundaries between actresses and aristocrats.[19]

Like Nell Gwyn, Margaret Hughes was one of the first actresses. Known for her beauty and theatrical talents, she became even more famous for being the mistress of the king's cousin Prince Rupert. Portraits of Gwyn and Hughes by Peter Lely resemble Lely's images of countesses and duchesses. In several pictures by members of Lely's studio, images of Gwyn in profile dressed in stylish gowns, wearing pearls, mimic Lely's portraits of Elizabeth Wriothesley, Countess of Northumberland (later Duchess of Montagu), and Anne Digby, Countess of Sunderland.[20] An elaborate portrait by Lely of Margaret Hughes depicts the actress seated in profile next to an ornately carved fountain (Figure 6). She holds a scallop shell in one hand to catch the streaming water, and a lemon in the other. She wears a pearl necklace, pearl earrings, and a long strand of pearls woven through her hair. The curators of the exhibit *Painted Ladies* note, "Once Prince Rupert had rid himself of his previous mistress, Frances Bard, he and Peg Hughes lived practically as man and wife. Something of the propriety of their relationship is referred to in Lely's fine portrait, in which

---

[17] MacLeod and Marciari Alexander, "'Windsor Beauties,'" pp. 81, 104.

[18] www.rct.uk/collection/404957/barbara-villiers-duchess-of-cleveland-ca-1641-1709.

[19] For more on Restoration actresses and their portraits, see MacLeod and Marciari Alexander, *Painted Ladies*; Perry, Roach, and West, *First Actresses*.

[20] MacLeod and Marciari Alexander, "'Windsor Beauties'," pp. 92–3.

Figure 6 *Margaret Hughes*, mezzotint by Robert Williams, after Sir Peter Lely, 1670s–80s. National Portrait Gallery

the sitter is depicted as a lady of quality, with no pictorial illusions to being either an actress or mistress."[21] The subsequent mezzotint, which allowed for even greater distribution of the image, clearly renders the composition.

Several portraits of Nell Gwyn as Venus highlight her nudity and sexuality while simultaneously presenting her as an idealized goddess. In an engraving titled *Nell Gywn and Her Two Sons* by Antoine Masson (after a portrait by Henri Gascar), circa 1677–80, Gwyn is reclining partially dressed on a bed of flora and silk wearing a prominent pearl necklace. Her sons, illegitimate children of the king, hover as naked cherubim above her, one holding a curtain in a gesture of theatrical unveiling, the other holding Cupid's arrow, as if to suggest his mother's role as Venus and his own birth as a product of seduction.[22] Perhaps the pearls are

---

[21]　Quoted in MacLeod and Marciari Alexander, *Painted Ladies*, p. 115.

[22]　The engraving can be viewed online: www.rct.uk/collection/themes/exhibitions/charles-ii-art-power/ the-queens-gallery-buckingham-palace/nell-gwyn-and-her-two-sons. As this Royal Collections Trust webpage informs us,

> Eleanor "Nell" Gywn was one of the first professional actresses on the London stage. She became Charles II's mistress in 1668 or 1669 and bore him two sons. This print celebrates Nell's fertility. Surrounded by plants, she reclines with her two sons depicted as cupids, while Charles II is shown across the lake dressed in Roman garb. An early pencil annotation

added here to identify Gwyn specifically, and/or to tie her directly to the court. Gwyn's role as Venus and as herself in this image conflates idealized images of her with the embodied reality of her intimate connection to the royal family. The print functions as both a pinup of Gwyn, another advertisement of her beauty, and as an important reminder of her connection to the king.

The pearls in Lely's painting of Margaret Hughes similarly echo a range of meanings that in fact reinforce the power of her identity as an actress to reimagine herself in another role. For Hughes, jewelry and pearls specifically became symbolic of her transformation from a stage actress to a powerful royal mistress. Prince Rupert gave Margaret an extraordinary pearl necklace that belonged to his mother, Elizabeth Stuart, Queen of Bohemia (often known as the Winter Queen). Nell Gwyn apparently borrowed and wore this piece of famed jewelry in the portrait of her by Simon Verelst (Figure 1) pictured in Section 1. Later in her life, to help settle her extensive gambling debts, Hughes sold the necklace to Gwyn, who bought it for an enormous sum.[23] The transference of pearls, both real and imagined, between these actresses who came from nothing, rose to prominence through their theatrical careers and strategic liaisons, and ultimately died in poverty, marks the tangible and symbolic trajectory of their celebrity.

1.4 Pearls and Empire

The tangible and visible celebrity of early actresses (and by extension Charles's mistresses), alongside their ability to insinuate themselves into the bedrooms and lives of powerful men, engendered a great deal of anxiety. Actresses could be dangerous foreign infiltrators capable of contaminating bloodlines and using their alluring exotic charms to divert wealth and resources from legitimate descendants. Pearls often appear in portraits of women as symbols of the foreign, enslaved, sexualized, and unknown, as well as emblems of whiteness, exoticism, empire, and global networks. Actresses were enmeshed in these trajectories – both in terms of their performances in plays like Dryden's *The Indian Queen* and in their associated characterization as foreign mysterious others.[24]

---

on this impression states that she is wearing a lace gown stolen from her main rival for Charles's affections, Louise de Kéroualle.

[23] According to Linda Porter, "Nell liked jewels as much as any society lady of the period and seems to have had a particular weakness for pearls … In 1682, after the death of Charles II's cousin, Prince Rupert, she paid over £4,000, or £644,000 today, for a pearl necklace that the Prince had given his mistress, Peg Hughes, herself an actress" (*Mistresses*, p. 161).

[24] For an excellent analysis of Anne Bracegirdle's parasol in a print of her as Semernia the Indian Queen in the play *The Widow Ranter*, as a protector of whiteness and as appropriated accessory, see Roach, *It*, pp. 166–7; L. Rosenthal, *Ways of the World*, pp. 136–7.

Figure 7 Louise de Kéroualle, *Duchess of Portsmouth with an Unknown Female Attendant*, by Pierre Mignard, 1682. National Portrait Gallery

Pierre Mignard's now-famous portrait of Louise de Kéroualle, Duchess of Portsmouth, the well-known French mistress of Charles II and a contemporary of Nell Gwyn's, depicts the beautifully dressed duchess in pearl earrings with her arm around a young black female servant, wearing a pearl choker and holding a conch shell of gleaming pearls in her hand (Figure 7). Set against a background of a distant sea, the image emphasizes the glory of conquest and maritime exploits, embodied by the duchess's ornate dress, regal pose, and translucent white skin. The enslaved figure gazes up at her mistress, the pearls around her neck highlighting her blackness and subjugation. She offers her mistress additional pearls as an extra signification of the depth of the duchess's wealth. Her presence in pearls further highlights the sustainment of the violent colonial practices that produced pearls as exchangeable commodities. For Kim Hall, this portrait helps us understand how pearls operate in conveying ideas about beauty, whiteness, and English identity:

> In using the servant's skin to accentuate her status, Portsmouth reinserts herself into a political economy of beauty ... In offering Portsmouth the objects that create beauty in metaphor, the Black attendant offers the spectator an affirmation of an English ideal. However, as the pose of the child suggests, that English ideal of the fair woman is generated and maintained by

the accumulation of goods. Coral and pearls are not just metaphors. They appear prominently in both domestic manuals and art treatises: the acquisition of these items figured prominently in English trade practices.[25]

Additionally, Warsh, in her analysis of the painting, contends that pearls are often explicitly linked to varied modes of enslavement: "The pearls here suggest the Duchess's slavish devotion – whether to luxury or to the king – by linking them to the enslaved child. The pearl collar on the female slave, worn as a choker rather than as a necklace, further suggests the blurring of the line between pearls as adornment and pearls as symbols of slavery."[26] In a sense, the fact that the duchess and the enslaved child *both* wear pearls creates an unexpected analogy between them.

Issues of enslavement, whiteness, and modes of idealized beauty are also present in a miniature portrait of Nell Gwyn by an anonymous artist that surfaced in 2011, which depicts Gwyn in low-cut white nightdress wearing pearls and making sausages. The figure of a young black boy stands behind her dressed in servant's livery with a metallic collar around his neck, a clear sign of his status as a possession. He stares up at her, like the young girl in the Duchess of Portsmouth painting who gazes at her mistress. Gwyn and the duchess both look directly out at the viewer and do not engage with the servants. According to the antiques expert Philip Mould, the portrait of Gwyn is "the most graphic contemporary portrayal of her sexual qualifications that we have found. What makes it so distinctive is that this is not a smutty doodle, but exquisitely crafted. One can only assume that it may have had an intimate purpose in the court circle."[27] Although we cannot know if this painting, which was intended for "private use," is a direct response to or reworking of Mignard's portrait, Gwyn and the duchess were well-established rivals, and there are some compelling parallels in the paintings that both connect and distinguish the women from each other. The duchess is dressed in a sumptuous gown of luxurious fabrics fastened with jewels, set against an idealized window overlooking the sea. Gwyn is barely clothed in a simple white gown. She is in an interior domestic space caught in the act of making sausage. Gwyn's performance is highly sexualized, and she is being watched by the enslaved boy behind her, which sets up a series of erotic gazes. Gwyn, like the boy, is also an object to be owned, an actress/mistress who has bought into sexual work. At the same time, Gwyn, with her characteristic pearls, can also be seen as having perhaps some control over her ability to enslave and seduce men through her performances. Gwyn's whiteness

---

[25] Hall, *Things of Darkness*, p. 253.   [26] Warsh, *American Baroque*, p. 222.

[27] Alberge, "Graphic Portrait of Charles II's Mistress Comes to Light." A higher-resolution version of the image can be viewed online: www.historicalportraits.com/Gallery.asp?Page=Item&ItemID=2233&Desc=Portrait-of-Nell-Gwyn-|–Anglo-Dutch-School.

in this image, highlighted by her dress, exposed skin, and accessory, are juxtaposed with the boy's blackness, suggesting that through her performances she is achieving an embodiment of feminized Englishness, although her status as an actress will always make her a foreign being, someone who has infiltrated a higher space from below. In comparison to the duchess, whose status and wealth is paramount in her portrait and whose enslaved servant wears pearls instead of a metal collar, Gwyn is presented as the counterfeit counterpart in a behind-the-scenes look at what really happens in the dark. Pearls signify Gwyn's role as an actress, a mistress, and an insidious infiltrator of domestic spaces – someone who is capable of sexual production that could destabilize a nation. Pearls are essential markers of meaning in both images, helping us understand the many ways actresses occupied a precarious and significant place in the early modern world.

1.5 Joan Carlile, Mary Beale, and Anne Killigrew: Self-Portraits and Pearls

Considering portraits of the early actresses Nell Gywn and Margaret Hughes alongside images of aristocrats and wealthy mistresses of the king presents an opportunity to think about how artists used pearls to highlight and complicate actresses' paradoxical power, beauty, and dangerous allure. But what does it mean when female artists use pearls as signifiers in their self-representations? Until recently very little attention has been paid to Restoration women painters Joan Carlile, Anne Killigrew (also a well-known poet), and Mary Beale. As Bendor Grosvenor, the curator of the beautiful exhibit *Bright Souls: The Forgotten Story of Britain's First Female Artists* (2019), reminds us, at the same moment that actresses appeared on the British stage, women artists were also emerging in and around the court:

> There had been professional women artists working in Britain in the 16th century, though these came from Europe, such as the miniaturist Levina Teerlinc of Flanders, where women enjoyed greater freedoms. But when it came to easel painting in oil, no British woman had ever attempted – or more likely, been allowed – to work professionally. The political upheavals in 17th-century Britain, however, so shook the traditional structures of society that just occasionally opportunities arose which allowed gifted amateur female painters to try their hand at painting for money.[28]

It is perhaps not surprising that these early painters – Joan Carlile, Mary Beale, and Anne Killigrew – all portrayed themselves in pearls.

---

[28] Grosvenor, *Bright Souls*, p. 4.

Joan Carlile (ca. 1606–79), the wife of an amateur playwright and poet, moved to London in her mid-forties with her six children to try to make a living as an artist. She settled in Covent Garden, the theater district and home to the studios of important artists such as Sir Peter Lely. Charles I eventually became her patron, and her surviving works suggest that she excelled at portraits of notable female aristocrats and families. Carlile's specialty seems to have been representing women in luxurious white dresses wearing pearls. Three portraits of aristocratic women from the 1650s feature figures in white silk dresses standing center stage against delicately rendered landscapes.[29] The dresses are nearly identical with characteristic mid-seventeenth-century low-cut bodices and puffed sleeves, trimmed with jewels at the neckline that draw attention to the subject's pearl necklaces, earrings, and hair ornaments. Grosvenor suggests that Carlile hit on a winning formula with these repeated representations.[30] Women clearly wished to see themselves styled with pearls in images that highlighted their role as wealthy, regal, lovely performers. Later in the century, white dresses would become synonymous with actresses' stage costumes.[31] Painting a white dress and gleaming accessories displays the skill of the artist in depicting shimmering fabrics and objects. Carlile was here also clearly echoing other contemporary artists such as Van Dyck, Lely, and Kneller.

In *The Carlile Family with Sir Justinian Isham in Richmond Park (The Stag Hunt)* (ca. 1650), Carlile depicts herself in a fashionable white gown and pearls, inserting herself as the artist, object/subject, alongside her family and another wealthy family (Figure 8). Here Carlile's artistic practice is legitimized and subsumed under the normal activities for English families. She enacts a performance of creative talent and disguise; she is the director of this scene as well as an actress on the stage of the canvas. Carlile's pearls and white dress echo the costume and accessories she designed for her portraits of wealthy women. The portrait is an advertisement for herself as an artist, as well as a statement of self-fashioning and creative legitimacy.

The artist Mary Beale (1633–99) is "credited with being the first successful woman artist."[32] By the late 1670s, her extensive list of patrons included aristocrats and royalty. Her husband, Charles, also her studio manager, kept detailed records of her transactions that still survive. Nell Gwyn became Mary

---

[29] See, for example, Carlile's *Portrait of an Unknown Lady,* circa 1650–5, online: www.tate.org.uk/art/artworks/carlile-portrait-of-an-unknown-lady-t14495.

[30] Grosvenor, *Bright Souls,* p. 14.

[31] For further discussion of white stage dresses, see Engel, *Women, Performance, and the Material of Memory,* pp. 34–8.

[32] Grosvenor, *Bright Souls,* p. 17.

Figure 8 Joan Palmer Carlile, *The Carlile Family with Sir Justinian Isham in Richmond Park*, 1650s. Kindly reproduced by permission of Lamport Hall Preservation Trust

Beale's neighbor in 1670, when Charles II set up a house for her and her new baby, the king's son who would become the Duke of St. Albans.[33] Beale painted Gwyn's portrait in 1676–7.[34] She portrays the young actress wearing a blue dress and pearls. Nothing about the portrait suggests Gwyn's identity as a theatrical performer. The simple strand of pearls around her neck can be read as a signifier of her status as a fashionable young woman. With her portrait of Gwyn, Beale seems to anticipate later artists such as Sir Joshua Reynolds, George Romney, and Thomas Lawrence, who often depicted actresses in portraits as "themselves." These images served as simultaneous advertisements for the female performer and the artist.

An early self-portrait of Beale dated 1660 depicts the artist posed with her family wearing pearls.[35] While Carlile's portrayal of herself is idealized – her

---

[33] Hunting, *My Dearest Heart*, pp. 133–4.

[34] Beale's portrait of Gwyn can be seen online: https://commons.wikimedia.org/wiki/File: Mary_Beale_(attr)_Portrait of Nell Gwyl.jpg.

[35] This Beale self-/family portrait can be viewed online: https://artuk.org/discover/artworks/self-portrait-of-mary-beale-with-her-husband-and-son-133035.

features and expression are like other faces in her portraits – Beale's depiction of herself is more specific and unique. She stands in profile and looks directly at the viewer while her husband watches her. Their son stands between them. Beale wears a fashionable but unadorned brown dress. Her pearl necklace and earrings are the only signifiers of wealth and prosperity in the painting. The whiteness of the pearls against Beale's bosom also draws the spectator's eye to her hand, which holds a piece of drapery across her shoulder. Perhaps Beale wanted to highlight the presence of her hand as a tool for her artistry. In this painting, pearls signify the agency and adornment of everyday professional women. She seems to be challenging the viewer to see her simultaneously as an artist and as a mother. This would be a strategy for gaining legitimacy later in the century for women artists such as Vigée Le Brun. A print of a self-portrait of Beale, now in the Lewis Walpole Library, depicts her wearing pearls and looking confidently at the spectator (Figure 9). Thus, it could be said that the afterlife of Beale's self-image is closely tied to pearls as a symbol of prosperity and status.

The poet and painter Anne Killigrew died very young of smallpox in 1685. Dryden wrote a now well-known ode to the young prodigy, which has received far more attention than Killigrew's own poetry and paintings.[36] Killigrew's

Figure 9 *Mrs. Beale the paintress, drawn by herself.* Courtesy of the Lewis Walpole Library, Yale University

---

[36] Only four portraits and twenty-five poems of Killigrew's survive (Grosvenor, *Bright Souls*, p. 30).

participation in these sister-arts establishes a compelling early trajectory that will resurface later in the careers of Angelica Kauffman and Anne Damer (the subjects of Section 2). Killigrew grew up at court surrounded by the royal art collections, music, theater, fashion, and jewels. Her father was the chaplain of the Church of England and her mother was a lady-in-waiting to the queen, Catherine of Braganza. Anne later became the maid of honor to Mary of Modena, the second wife of James, the Duke of York. Her contemporaries included Anne Finch and Sarah Jennings, the Duchess of Marlborough, a specific favorite of Queen Anne. Further, there is the possibility of a direct link between Killigrew and Joan Carlile. Grosvenor suggests that Killigrew might actually have been taught by Carlile, and he highlights the theatrical connections between the two families: "We can with reasonable certainty assume that the Killigrews and Carliles were acquainted: they lived very close to each other near Whitehall; both were involved with the royal household; and as a playwright, Lodowick Carlile worked with Dryden, and must have known both Thomas and William Killigrew, Anne's playwright uncles."[37]

In a 1685 self-portrait, she stands center stage again wearing pearls, dressed in a luxurious gown with a black bodice, white sleeves, and a red silk skirt with a floral pattern.[38] In her hand she clasps a piece of paper, perhaps signifying her role as an author/poet. Behind her are ornate stone sculptures with meticulously rendered scenes of women – a woman with a child on the tablet to her right and a female goddess figure, perhaps Diana or Minerva, on the pedestal of the sculpture to her left. The set of the portrait is framed by curtains that reveal a landscape in the background. While there are some similarities between Killigrew's and Carlile's compositions – both artists center their subjects against idealized landscapes – Killigrew's self-portraits are dramatic representations of her identity in different guises. Killigrew's attention to detail suggests her desire to portray herself as a serious artist capable of copying master works while producing her own interpretation of classical subject matter. Presenting herself as an accomplished artist and author in a royal setting, wearing pearls, Killigrew highlights her creativity, genius, and status.

---

[37] Ibid., p. 32. From here, Grosvenor continues with further support for this contention: "Another tantalising lost painting described by George Vertue could yet be revealing: 'Mrs. Carlile taught a Lady . . . to draw & paint. & drew her own picture setting with a book of drawings on her lap. & this Lady Standing behind her. This picture was in posses. of Mr Carlile in Westminster.' Was the 'Lady' Anne?" (ibid.).

[38] This Killigrew self-portrait can be viewed online: https://commons.wikimedia.org/wiki/File: Anne_Killigrew_(British_1660-1685)-_Self-Portrait.jpg.

In an even more striking image, another self-portrait, circa 1685, Killigrew depicts herself in a pastoral setting, perhaps inspired by her performance in Anne Finch's court masque *Venus and Adonis*, for which she wore pearls.[39] Unlike the somewhat more somber depictions in the previous paintings, Killigrew's costume here is a vibrant pink trimmed with white. Her sandaled foot peeks out from beneath her skirt; she gazes tentatively at the viewer, her pearl necklace and earrings highlighting the whiteness of her skin. Grosvenor further speculates that Killigrew's allegorical painting *Venus Attired by the Graces* may have been created in honor of Mary of Modena, who was referred to as a "Modern Day Venus."[40] Killigrew there represents Venus and her attendant with pearls in their hair. Killigrew's references to Venus, highlighted by her use of pearls, signals her participation in the Venus-inspired culture of female beauty, power, and performance at court. Her playful adoption of roles to promote her own image establishes important connections among visual, narrative, and theatrical modes of self-fashioning. A posthumous print of Killigrew, after a portrait by Peter Lely published in 1821, portrays the artist wearing pearls (Figure 10). As in the self-portrait of Mary Beale circulated after her death, the afterlife of Killigrew's image is also connected to pearls. Like Carlile and Beale, Killigrew's choice to present herself in pearls suggests the variety of meanings and modalities the accessory could convey to Restoration audiences. As early female artists, these women also performed as actresses, placing their own bodies on display for audiences, selling versions of themselves to spectators. Pearls connect Carlile, Beale, and Killigrew's self-portraits to depictions of actresses, mistresses, and royal women by accomplished male artists, while simultaneously emphasizing the links between these subjects and the artists themselves. The art of the actress, then, can also be extended to the performances of female artists, who may have been channeling some of the allure, mystique, and agency that Nell Gwyn and other Restoration performers embodied on- and offstage.[41]

---

[39] Winn, *Queen Anne: Patroness of Arts*, p. 105. According to Winn, Finch directed that Killigrew perform a live tableau to accompany this moment in John Blow's libretto: "While the graces dance, the cupids dress Venus, one combing her head, another ties a bracelet of pearls round her wrist." This reenactment involving self-fashioning with pearls echoes the lines in Aphra Behn's poem "Pindarick Poem on the Coronation," "And in the flowing jetty curles / They weave and braid the luced pearls" (ibid.). This self-portrait can be viewed online: https://commons.wikime dia.org/wiki/File:Anne_Killigrew,_Portrait_of_a_Lady,_Private_Collection,_Scotland.jpg.

[40] Grosvenor, *Bright Souls*, p. 35. The *Venus Attired by the Graces* painting can be seen online: https://commons.wikimedia.org/wiki/File:Anne_Killigrew_-_Venus_Attired_by_the_Three_ Graces.jpg.

[41] See also a print made by Abraham Blooteling (1640–90) of Anne Killigrew's self-portrait in the Yale Center for British Art. She wears pearl earrings and her dress is decorated with pearls: https://collections.britishart.yale.edu/catalog/tms:51044.

Figure 10 *Anne Killigrew,* by Francis Engleheart, after Sir Peter Lely, stipple engraving, 1821. National Portrait Gallery

1.6 Pearls and Paste: The Afterlives of Stage Pearls

While pearls remained fashionable accessories in portraits of royalty and aristocrats into the eighteenth century, particularly in the 1770s, images of actresses in pearls reached new heights in the 1780s with a lavish portrait of the celebrated actress Elizabeth Farren (*Elizabeth Farren as Hermione in The Winter's Tale,* ca. 1780) by Johan Zoffany (Figure 11), as well as the legendary *Sarah Siddons as the Tragic Muse* by Sir Joshua Reynolds (1784) (Figure 12).[42] Zoffany's full-length portrayal of Farren as Hermione in *The Winter's Tale* presents the actress leaning on a stone pedestal wearing a sumptuous white

---

[42] Perhaps Zoffany was inspired by Angelica Kauffman's 1775 portrait of the actress Elizabeth Hartley as Hermione: https://commons.wikimedia.org/wiki/File:Elizabeth_Hartley_by_ Angelica_Kauffmann.jpg. Although Hartley is not wearing pearls therein, the curtain, stone pedestal, and costume prefigure Zoffany's portrayal of Farren. This painting is also compelling when compared to Kauffman's later portraits of performing women, and her own self-portrait of 1787 discussed in Section 2. For more on this painting, see Perry, *Spectacular Flirtations,* p. 32.

Figure 11 *Elizabeth Farren as Hermione in The Winter's Tale* (ca. 1780), by
Johan Joseph Zoffany. National Gallery of Victoria

silk dress with a gold underskirt, trimmed with gleaming jewels and pearls.
Around her neck is a richly layered necklace of multiple strands of pearls. She
poses in mid-action at the moment in Shakespeare's play when Hermione
transforms from stone and comes back to life. Her hand holds up
a transparent veil kept in place by a gold crown. She looks directly at the viewer
with an expression of subdued melancholy. Farren's gown, pearls, and luxurious
adornments suggest an idealized version of a stage costume. Zoffany was
known for his theatrical portraits and excelled at capturing the idea of a scene
or character using his own interpretation of the setting and staging, and as Robin
Simon suggests, "Zoffany's nuanced approach enabled him to create
a distinctive effect: that of depicting the actors both in and out of character at
the same time."[43] His painting of Farren is as much about Farren the beautiful

---

[43] Simon, "Strong Impressions of Their Art," pp. 52, 59.

Figure 12 *Sarah Siddons (née Kemble) as the Tragic Muse*, stipple by Francis Haward, after Sir Joshua Reynolds, published 1787. National Portrait Gallery

celebrity as it is about Farren in the lofty role of Hermione, a part passed down to her from the legendary actress Hannah Pritchard.

A print of Pritchard in the character of Hermione presents the actress wearing a distinctive pearl necklace attached to a crucifix (Figure 13). While we do not know if the image is a direct copy of what Pritchard wore onstage, we can assume that actresses did wear jewelry (likely fake, or, if real, borrowed from wealthy friends or patrons) and that pearls may have been associated with specific roles. Zoffany's idea of Hermoine on the stage may have been influenced by Pritchard's performances. Pritchard is wearing a more demure strand of pearls around her neck and woven through her hair in Zoffany's portrait of her as Lady Macbeth (1768). Elaborate pearls, similar to the necklace Zoffany's Farren wears, appear in Sir Joshua Reynolds's famous portrait *Sarah Siddons As the Tragic Muse* (1784). Although much has been written about this portrait as

Figure 13 *Mrs. Pritchard in the Character of Hermione in The Winter's Tale*,
print by Simon François Ravenet, and by François-Germain Aliamet, after
Robert Edge Pine line engraving, published 1765. National Portrait Gallery

emblematic of Siddons's unparalleled celebrity, her connection to tragedy, the
sublime, nationalism, pallor/whiteness, and the mythologizing of female per-
formers, very little attention has been paid to her pearls.[44] The pearls in the
Tragic Muse portrait are truly ornate; there are compelling similarities between
Farren's pearls, Pritchard's pearls, and the pearls Siddons wears as the Tragic
Muse.

Although Siddons does not represent Hermoine in this image, appearing as
the Tragic Muse, a goddess of theater and a mythological figure, associates her
with the idea of sculpture and lasting iconic memory. Fiona Shen's discussion of
Sarah Siddons's pearls in Reynolds's *The Tragic Muse* more specifically

---

[44] For discussions of Siddons and portraiture, particularly the pallor of her skin and fashion, see
Asleson, *Passion for Performance*; Engel, *Fashioning Celebrity*; Freeman, "Mourning the
'Dignity of the Siddonian Form'"; MacPherson, *Art and Celebrity*, pp. 101–26; Roach, *It*,
pp. 146–73.

emphasizes potential ties to melancholy and their value as now-lost material objects. She writes, "No comparable necklace has ever been unearthed, though it may have been lost in an 1808 fire in Covent Garden Theatre which incinerated Siddons's professional costumes and jewelry too."[45] The accessory thus gestures toward the realism of what Siddons might have worn onstage, at the same time that its ornate, unreal qualities suggest a fictional or fantastical version of Siddons as a concept. As the Tragic Muse in the painting, Siddons is a statue, a personification come to life on canvas. Siddons's pearls in Reynolds's portrait are an amalgam of Farren's layered multiple strands of pearls and Pritchard's pearls attached to a crucifix. In Reynolds's portrait of Siddons, the multiple strands of pearls connect to form a crucifix shape. Looking closely at depictions of pearls in images of these three iconic actresses offers a connecting thread between actresses' performances and the range of fantasies and desires circulating around them. By this point in the eighteenth century, actresses had come a long way from the anxieties the dazzling early performers Nell Gwyn and Margaret Hughes engendered. Yet the mysterious and often paradoxical resonance of pearls in images of actresses highlights important themes connected to the art of the actress: is the art of the actress ephemeral or permanent, authentic or constructed, real or imagined?

2 The Actress As Artist and the Artist As Actress: Anne Damer and Angelica Kauffman

Although the theatrical critic William Hazlitt rapturously described Sarah Siddons's performances as "Tragedy personified,"[46] elevating her craft to an art form by the end of the eighteenth century, the idea of the actress as an artist did not become pervasive until the mid-nineteenth century, when Sarah Bernhardt fashioned herself as both an actress and a sculptress.[47]

Yet the connections between artists and actresses extend back to eighteenth-century practices. For female artists, performing the role of artist, creator, and muse required a very clever and strategic sense of acting. For actresses, visualizing themselves as artistic creations and fashioning themselves as beautiful objects became part of the trajectory of successful careers. In this section, I look closely at two women whose artistic productions were shaped by their experiences as actresses and artists. Angelica Kauffman became one of the first

---

[45] Shen, *Pearls*, p. 8. See also Skyler Sunday's master's thesis, "Rendering Documentary Portraiture," for a wonderful discussion of the shadow box that contains a pearl necklace that belonged to Sarah Siddons (now in the Harvard Library Theatre Collection).

[46] Quoted in Freeman, "Mourning the 'Dignity of the Siddonian Form,'" p. 598.

[47] For more about Sarah Bernhardt as a sculptress, see Ockman et al., *Sarah Bernhardt*, pp. 43–4. Sarah Siddons learned to sculpt from Anne Damer, but was not a professional visual artist. See Gross, *Life of Anne Damer*, p. 163.

women accepted into the Royal Academy and enjoyed enormous fame across Europe in the second part of the eighteenth century. Known for her dramatic history paintings, fashionable and allegorical portraits of women, and extraordinary self-portraits, Kauffman continuously returned to the dramatization and effects of female performances throughout her career.[48] One of her first commissions when she arrived in England in 1766, after studying art in Italy, was a portrait of Anne Seymour Conway (later Damer), a lovely young aristocrat about to be married. The painting of Damer as Ceres, dressed in a stylish pastoral gown with a crown of leaves, flowers, and pearls in her hair (Figure 14), only hints at the accomplished sculptress, actress, and novelist

Figure 14 *Hon. Anne Damer*: From an original in the possession of Right Honble. Genl. Conway/A. Kauffman R. A. pinxt., T. Ryder sculpt. 1793. Courtesy of the Lewis Walpole Library, Yale University

---

[48] Central studies on Angelica Kauffman include A. Rosenthal, *Angelica Kauffman*; Baumgärtel, ed., *Angelica Kauffman*; Roworth, ed., *Angelica Kauffman*; Spies-Gans, *Revolution on Canvas*.

Damer would become after her disastrous marriage to John Damer, a career gambler who eventually committed suicide. Along with Mary and Agnes Berry and Diana Beauclerk, Damer enjoyed the patronage and admiration of her cousin the author and art collector Horace Walpole, whose extraordinary gothic house, Strawberry Hill, she inherited after his death.[49] Damer's sculptures of prominent actresses, aristocrats, and royalty, as well as her meticulously crafted dogs, made her a celebrated and threatening figure. In addition to her talents as an artist, Damer starred in private theatricals she helped coordinate and stage, including decorating the sets with her artworks. Dressed in elaborate costumes accessorized with expensive jewels, Damer appeared as an art object herself, dazzling spectators with her beauty and style.[50] Kauffman was similarly celebrated for her loveliness. When the Danish ambassador in London famously declared that the world had gone "Angelica Mad," it was as much about the stunning quality of her artworks as it was about the artistic persona she had crafted for herself. Both women appeared as living muses.

Although Kauffman and Damer had different professional trajectories and worked in different media, their parallel lives and careers offer important insight into the simultaneous roles enacted by the female artist and actress in the latter half of the eighteenth century. Damer and Kauffman are often mentioned together in studies on eighteenth-century women artists and artistic female celebrities, but very little work has been done on the echoes between their subject matter or the personal connections that may have informed their practices.[51] While Kauffman was not the only artist involved in making a series of self-portraits in different guises or to feature actresses and singers in her portraits, she had a unique connection to performance. Kauffman began her career as a singer and represented the duality of performance versus other artistic pursuits in several of her paintings.[52] Damer's close friendships with the actresses Eliza Farren and Sarah Siddons influenced her artistic practice as well as her career as an actress in private theatricals. She made busts of both women, and Siddons and Farren assisted in her performance at Richmond House, where she fashioned the stage with representations of her favorite female muses.[53]

---

[49] For more on the women artists of Strawberry Hill, see Roman, "Art of Lady Diana Beauclerk."

[50] There are two recent biographies of Anne Damer: Gross, *Life of Anne Damer*; Webb, *Mrs D*. See also Noble, *Anne Seymour Damer*.

[51] Though scant attention has been paid to the connections between Damer and Kauffman specifically, much has been written on the history of eighteenth-century women artists, networks, and collaboration – see the following germinal works: Hyde and Milam, *Women, Art, and the Politics of Identity in Eighteenth-Century Europe*; Sherriff, "Pour l'histoire des femmes artistes"; Spies-Gans, *Revolution on Canvas*; Strobel, *Artistic Matronage of Queen Charlotte*.

[52] See Brylowe, "Angelica Kauffman and the Sister Arts."

[53] For a discussion of Damer's artworks in performance, see Engel "Stage Beauties"; Tuite, "Comedy, Too Fatal Emblem."

Damer later exchanged roles with Farren; she played the countess in the private theatrical performance of her father's play *False Appearances*. Farren reprised the role at Drury Lane the following season. Kauffman and Damer both had close associations with Emma Hamilton, the creator of a performance series based on attitudes or sculptures come to life, and the mistress of Lord Nelson.[54] (I'll return to Kauffman's vibrant portrait of Hamilton later in this section.) Damer attempted to further promote her career by sculpting a bust of Lord Nelson, which she hoped would appear on the frontispiece of his biography.[55]

In addition to performing versions of themselves in various artworks, both women had to continuously negotiate the demands of their public performances and visible celebrity. Kauffman's general success at promoting herself relied on crafting attractive and accessible personae that allied themselves with available and idealized modes of femininity and female identity. Yet the tensions and shifting nature of these personae, even within the images themselves, suggests the constructed nature of her performances. Damer's role in the public eye became far more vexed, due in part to her close relationships with women as well as her unconventional modes of dress and choice of media. A female sculptress is inextricably tied to the creation of three-dimensional bodies, yet women were prohibited from studying anatomy – the idea of a female making a male body threatened established notions of artistic practice and creativity based on the model of the male artist and female object. Damer and Kauffman revised the myth of Pygmalion, performing both the roles of Pygmalion and Galatea.

Damer's and Kauffman's representations of themselves as well as other female subjects as fluid and artful presents a unique view of the art of the actress. Femininity itself is a fluctuating category of identity that echoes the ephemerality and mutability of performance. The idea of the actress as an artist and the artist as an actress highlights contradictions and tensions inherent in the dynamics of public presentation and self-fashioning, particularly for women in the latter part of the eighteenth century. As Angela Rosenthal reminds us, "To understand how a female portraitist in the eighteenth century could achieve such a powerful cultural presence, it is useful to address the apparent contradiction she embodies, between a domestic art of mimesis and a dangerous indecorous visuality."[56] Women participating the public realm of the arts necessitated strategies of self-fashioning that aligned their personas with idealized qualities of femininity at odds with the practices of display and self-promotion.

---

[54] For more on Emma Hamilton's attitudes, see Rauser, "Living Statues and Neoclassical Dress in Late Eighteenth-Century Naples."

[55] Noble, *Anne Seymour Damer*, pp. 156–8.   [56] A. Rosenthal, *Angelica Kauffman*, 48.

Damer's and Kauffman's use of specific iconography including classical motifs, personas, and masks, as well as accessories associated with artistic practice, underscores their continuous oscillation between the roles of artist and subject. Sculpture is a static but three-dimensional format; painting is two-dimensional but can record movement. Kauffman incorporated sculpture into her paintings, often to emphasize the lofty and lasting qualities of herself and/or her female subjects. Damer used her sculptures in performance, juxtaposing the dynamics of actresses' artistic agency with the legacy of their visual presence. Kauffman and Damer both provide particularly resonant examples of artists working across media collaboratively and inspired by other female artists. For Angela Rosenthal, Kauffman's work is all about the concept of "intersubjectivity" or the "encounters between artist and subject." According to Rosenthal, "what distinguishes portraiture from other genres of representation is its dependence on the (real or imagined) personal encounter between artist and sitter. Not merely a reproduction of a preexisting self, the act of portrayal is seen here as bringing subjectivities into being."[57] Looking at Kauffman's and Damer's work together invites the following questions: How do Kauffman and Damer enact forms of subjectivity and intersubjectivity? How do they focus our attention on a range of female identities and their relationship(s) to one another? How are their artworks documents of what Rosenthal describes as "being and becoming"?[58]

2.1 The Performance of Self-Portraits

For Angelica Kauffman and Anne Damer, the inextricable relationship between artistic practice and performance is evident in the ways in which they represented themselves. Kauffman's many self-portraits dramatize the relationship between the act of being an artist and the multifaceted meanings of appearing as oneself. Her inclusion of references to various media, sculpture, jewelry, and fashion link these varied images to models of female identity often based on the muses of mythology. Damer's aesthetic, drawn from antique sculpture, emphasized the idealized beauty and serenity of her female subjects. Her own 1778 self-portrait, emblazoned with an inscription in Greek, "Anne Seymour Damer from Britain. Made by Herself," echoes her sculptures of other women who inspired her, particularly the actress Elizabeth Farren and the playwright Mary Berry.[59] In contrast to the elegant pathos and solemnity of her portrait busts, Damer's theatrical performances were characterized by her lively wit, blazing

---

[57] A. Rosenthal, *Angelica Kauffman*, p. 4.   [58] Ibid.

[59] This sculpture can be viewed online: https://en.wikipedia.org/wiki/File:Anne_Seymour_ Damer_self-portrait.JPG.

jewelry, and seductive charm. The cosmopolitan heroines she excelled at playing, such as the countess in *False Appearances* (reprised by the actress Eliza Farren) and Lady Selina in Mary Berry's *Fashionable Friends* (reprised unsuccessfully by Dorothy Jordan), mirror her unconventional status as a female artist and independent widow. The tension between Damer's art forms – the memorialized beauty of sculpture and the shimmering presence of performance – is similar to the pull Kauffman dramatizes between painting and singing. In addition, Damer's and Kauffman's involvement in the "art of the actress" evokes a legacy of female relationships centered on the entanglements of public and private performances. These portraits and performances highlight female collaboration, network, genius, celebrity, and inspiration.

While all of Kauffman's self-portraits dramatize the act of posing and role-playing, a series of portraits that she completed in the 1790s in Rome highlight the pull she experienced between artistic media and theatrical expression. With her majestic 1791–4 *Self-Portrait of the Artist Hesitating between the Arts of Music and Painting*, Kauffman establishes her unequivocal claim to fame and the legitimacy of her artistic celebrity.[60] According to Bettina Baumgärtel, the painting represents a crucial turning point in her life, the decision to pursue painting over a career as a singer.[61] In fact, Kauffman's first portrait of herself, completed when she was twelve years old (1753), depicts the young artist in theatrical costume holding a sheet of music.[62] The image is a close view of her face and upper torso, a snapshot of her performative persona on canvas. Almost forty years later, a seasoned and well-known Kauffman stages her early dilemma as a history portrait that echoes the common use of traditional iconographic portrayals of Hercules at the crossroads between Virtue and Vice.[63] In this later painting, a lovely Kauffman stands poised between the female figures of Art and Music; one holds a scroll of music, the other a palette with paint. Kaufmann's fashionable white dress and golden accessories highlight her as the mortal presence in the scene. She clasps Music's hand tightly while simultaneously gesturing with an open palm toward Art. The decision is presented as heartfelt and serious, but even as it is clear what choice Kauffman is making, she holds fast to Music, emphasizing her affinity and connection for the art of

---

[60] Kauffman's *Self-Portrait of the Artist Hesitating between the Arts of Music and Painting* can be seen online: www.nationaltrustcollections.org.uk/object/960079.

[61] Baumgärtel, *Angelica Kauffman*, p. 40. Baumgärtel also here contends that Kauffman's choice to pursue painting over music aligned her with professionalism and virtue.

[62] Kauffman's early *Self-Portrait As a Singer with Sheet Music* can be viewed online: https://useum.org/artwork/Self-portrait-with-a-sheet-of-music-Angelica-Kauffman-1753.

[63] For example, Baumgärtel compares Kauffman's portrait to Sir Joshua Reynolds's 1761 painting *David Garrick between Comedy and Tragedy* (p. 41).

Figure 15 *Lady Hamilton As the Comic Muse Thalia*, 1791. Raphael Morghen (1758–1833) after Angelica Kauffman. National Portrait Gallery

performance. In this way, Kauffman participates in legitimizing the art of performance for women as well as its ties to modes of aesthetic representation.

Kauffman further asserts her affinity for female theatrical performers with three portraits she completed during the period when she was working on the two versions of her self-portrait at the crossroads between art and music. Her 1791 *Lady Hamilton As the Comic Muse, Thalia* (Figure 15), her 1792 portrait of the *Impromptu Virtuoso Fortunata Sulger Fantastici* (Figure 16), along with the 1794 *Portrait of the Impromptu Virtuoso Teresa Bandettini Landucci As Muse*, form a unique gallery of beauties based on the dynamics and skill of acting.[64] Emma Hamilton, known for her theatrical attitudes, a series of performances that brought antique sculpture to life, in fact became a close associate of Kauffman's. Her celebrated beauty and attachment to Lord Nelson made her a particularly smart choice for Kauffman's brand.[65] Fantastici and Bandettini, Italian *improvvisatrici*, amazed audiences with their impromptu poetic skill and

---

[64] Kauffman's *Portrait of the Impromptu Virtuoso Teresa Bandettini-Landucci* can be viewed online: https://en.wikipedia.org/wiki/File:Angelika_Kauffmann_-_Portrait_of_the_Impromptu Virtuoso_Teresa_Bandettini-Landucci_of_Lucca_-_Google_Art_Project.jpg.

[65] For more on Kauffman's branding and celebrity, see Vickery, "Branding Angelica."

Figure 16 Angelica Kauffman, *Portrait of the Impromptu Virtuoso Fortunata Sulger Fantastici*, 1792. Florence, Palais Pitti, Galerie Palatine. Courtesy of AKG Images/Rabatti & Domingie

delivery. Fantastici became Kauffman's close friend. She wrote poems dedicated to the artist praising her talents and angelic nature.[66] Kauffman kept a copy of her portrait of Fantastici along with a miniature of her in her studio. As Serena Baiesi reminds us, there are important differences between Italian improvisational poets and actresses. Female poets were considered extemporaneous geniuses and divinely inspired. The *improvvisatrici* performed for "private" audiences and salons to avoid the stigma of being female on a public stage. Emma Hamilton's attitudes also aligned with private theatricals and forms of amateur entertainment. Kauffman's choice of subjects associates her own art with theatrical improvisation and authentic inspiration rather than professional skill. Representing these women as muses offered Kauffman a way to contextualize her own artistic performances and her role as an artist/actress within these legitimizing parameters.[67]

The portraits of Fantastici and Bandettini are echoes of one another in size and content. Considering them together creates a visual conversation between the two interrelated images. Fantastici appears in a white neoclassical gown

---

[66] See Baumgärtel, *Angelica Kauffman*, pp. 172–5, for more about Kauffman's friendship with Fantastici and the poems she wrote and dedicated to her.

[67] See Baiesi, "Influence of the Italian *Improvvisatrici* on British Romantic Women Writers," pp. 181–91.

Figure 17 *Self-Portrait As the Muse of Painting*, by Angelica Kauffman, 1787. Uffizi Gallery. Courtesy of AKG Images/Rabatti & Domingie

with a contrasting blue shawl and green turban trimmed with gold. Around her waist, she wears an elaborate belt fastened with a cameo featuring a sculptural relief of a standing figure. But these images also contain elements of Kauffman's full-length portrait of herself as the muse of painting from 1787, fashioned specifically for the Uffizi Gallery (Figure 17). Here, Kauffman wears a belt similar to the one in her Fantastici painting. Kauffman's depiction of her full body, posed with the tools of painting against an idealized classical background, holding a stylus in one hand and a drawing board in the other, emphasizes her simultaneous performance of artistic genius and ideal beauty.[68] Broadly, Kauffman's dress, accessories, expression, gestures, and cameo belt echo details of *both* the Fantastici and Bandettini portraits. Together they form a series of classical statues come to life, full-bodied enactments of artistic practice. The intricacies of Kauffman's portraits – her careful rendering of the gold embroidered trimming of Bandettini's dress, the minute attention to the cameo at the center of Fantastici's belt featuring a sculpture of a female figure – invite comparisons to Kauffman's portrayal of herself as an artist. The performative effect of these resonances underscores the inextricable connections

---

[68] Baumgärtel, *Angelica Kauffman*, p. 56.

between the artist as actress and the actress as artist. Kauffman's portrait of Emma Hamilton can also be considered part of this grouping. Kauffman's portrait of Hamilton is also full-length and almost life-sized. She is similarly dressed in an all-antica gown with an ornate belt featuring a cameo, holding a mask in one hand and a theatrical curtain in the other.

Kauffman's portrayal of Hamilton as Thalia, the muse of comedy, connects her to a legacy of classical sculpture as well as to the newly established world of female celebrity. According to Angela Rosenthal,

> Kauffman, without insisting on victory, compares painting and sculpture. But the artistic conceit runs deeper. For Hart [Lady Hamilton] and Kauffman approach mimesis from alternate positions, meeting as it were in the painting. Hart seeks to replicate art; Kauffman strives to capture Hart's transformation as a living sculpture while retaining the reference to the sitter's "real" identity. As Hart sweeps away the curtain, producing dramatic immediacy, Kauffman also presents a revelation, staging the fiction of an immediate view of her breathing subject.[69]

These portraits of Hamilton, Fantastici, and Bandettini suggest that the tool of the actress's art is her own body. Her expression, costume, and gesture all convey carefully crafted performances designed to move audiences in specific ways. In capturing these "moments," perhaps drawn from life or from memory, Kauffman pays homage to the intangible labor of actresses and to the lasting effects of their artistry through her own aesthetic practices and extraordinary skill.

Although Anne Damer's life and art have recently been receiving the attention they deserve, research and writing about Damer tends to focus on her identity as a sculptress along with her complex relationship with Mary Berry and her ties to queer histories. Scholars have discussed her appearance in private theatricals and her involvement in the Georgian social world but have not fully considered the ways her role as an actress can also be seen as a vital component of her artistry.[70] Except for a few volumes of her notebooks, Damer destroyed much of her private correspondence. We have very little information from Damer about her artistic practices or her strategies for performing a variety of featured roles in private performances. Putting together pieces of contemporary descriptions of her portrayals, costumes, and accessories, alongside images of her possibly drawn from or inspired by her performances, and the dynamics of the parts that she played, offers compelling ways of thinking about Damer's art

---

[69] A. Rosenthal, *Angelica Kauffman*, p. 187. NB: Before marrying Sir William Hamilton, Emma Hamilton went by the name Emma Hart.

[70] For more on Damer's reputation, artistic practice, and private theatricals, see Elfenbein, "Lesbian Aestheticism"; Tuite, "Comedy, Too Fatal Emblem."

as an actress as well as the ways in which her performative artistry may have been reflected and echoed in her sculptures. In addition, Damer's collaboration with Mary Berry on the creation and performance of Berry's play *Fashionable Friends*, performed initially as a private theatrical at Strawberry Hill, provides an ironic sense of Damer's awareness of herself as an ambiguous and misunderstood performer.[71]

Damer's performances in the celebrated Richmond Theatricals, a highly publicized series of plays that occurred during the spring season of 1787–8 at Richmond House, Privy Gardens, Whitehall, offered her an opportunity to design herself as an object of beauty and fascination for audiences comprised of aristocrats, royalty, and some of the leading actresses of the moment, Damer's personal friends Sarah Siddons and Eliza Farren. The first play performed was Arthur Murphy's *The Way to Keep Him*, and according to the theater historian Sybil Rosenfeld, "It was probably the first time that Mrs. Damer acted, though she was to become one of the most celebrated amateurs and to have theatricals in her own house at Strawberry Hill."[72] In a spoken epilogue to Murphy's play, newly written for Damer by her father, Damer connects acting to her identity as a sculptress:

> Oh, cou'd my humble skill, which often strove
> In mimic Stone to copy forms I love,
> By soft gradation reach a higher art,
> And bring to view a Sculpture of the heart.[73]

In a traditionally apologetic mode, Damer laments the difficulty of truly capturing "forms" that she loves through stone, suggesting in a slightly veiled way that acting onstage offers a more immediate opportunity to mimic the identities of her female muses. Her performances are then "a sculpture of the heart," a goal that diffuses the deceit and manipulation associated with actresses and emphasizes instead the sympathy and sentimentality of being inspired to "copy" beautiful forms – an acceptable role for a female artist.

Although Damer was often praised for the quality of her performances, she became best known for her dazzling, over-the-top costumes. A description of Damer's stage dress in her role as Athenias in the tragedy *Theodosius* in the May 12, 1788, *Gazetteer* creates an image of a fantastical work of art:

> The elegance of taste shewn in Mrs. Damer's last new stage dress beggars all description, and can only be excelled at by the attractive graces of the beautiful

---

[71] See the online exhibit *Artful Nature: Fashion and Theatricality*, curated by Engel and Rauser, for an extended discussion of *Fashionable Friends*: https://onlineexhibits.library.yale.edu/s/artful nature/page/intro.

[72] Rosenfeld, *Temples of Thespis*, p. 36.   [73] Quoted in Rosenfeld, *Temples of Thespis*, p. 39.

wearer. The petticoat was of celestial blue crepe spotted with silver, ornamented with wreaths of primroses, which were looped up with bows of diamonds; a festoon of primroses went round the bottom of the petticoat, finished with a rich silver fringe. The train was primrose coloured goffree'd crepe spotted with blue crepe in relief. The belt around the waist was of diamonds, with three diamond breast bows, and sleeve bows. The head-dress consisted only of a wreath of primroses, and a wreath of diamond lilies, surmounted by a panache of white, blue and primrose feathers.[74]

The observer notes that the dress, itself a work of art, adorned with flowers, diamonds, silver, as well as a headdress with multicolored feathers, is only surpassed by the beauty of Damer herself. Given the fact that Damer designed her own costumes (with possible help from Sarah Siddons, according to the famous actor John Kemble), it is important to highlight her dress as an act of self-curation and fashioning.[75] More than representing herself as an icon of style and wealth, Damer designs herself as an art object in performance, the reverse of Kauffman who captures performative moments on canvas. Damer becomes a living painting, an embodied fashion plate on stage. A watercolor of Damer painted by Harriet Carr (Figure 18), completed in the same year as the Richmond House Theatricals and now in the National Museum of Scotland, depicts Damer in a less-elaborate gown accessorized with a blue bejeweled sash and headdress and pearls, dancing toward the viewer. She holds an artist's tool in one hand and gestures toward a sculpture with the other. While this is not as formal a composition as Kauffman's representation of herself as torn between art and music, Carr's portrayal of Damer suggests that she is both a performer and a sculptress. In a painting of Damer by Sir Joshua Reynolds (in a private collection), Damer is supposedly represented as Athenias, a role originated by the Restoration actress Elizabeth Barry, in the final act where she was dressed in an imperial robe "of purple on a straw coloured bodice with an embroidery of flowers and was decorated with silver and ermine."[76] Reynolds's portrait of Damer in a deep-red gown trimmed in ermine fur, staring confidently at the viewer, echoes his portraits of the actress Frances Abington as Prue and the well-known courtesan Kitty Fisher completed in 1759. In both portraits, widely discussed by scholars, Abington and Fisher confront the viewer with an unwavering look, conveying their power as seductive theatrical performers as well as their availability to the spectator.[77] In echoing these images, Reynolds clearly saw Damer as a formidable theatrical persona in her own right.

---

[74] Quoted in Rosenfeld, *Temples of Thespis*, p. 50.   [75] Rosenfeld, *Temples of Thespis*, p. 50.

[76] Quoted in Rosenfeld, *Temples of Thespis*, p. 50.

[77] On Reynolds's portrait of Kitty Fisher as Cleopatra, see Pointon, *Brilliant Effects*, pp. 120–4; Perry, *Spectacular Flirtations*, pp. 40–1; Mudge, "Enchanting *Witchery*." For Frances Abington as Prue, see Perry, *Spectacular Flirtations*, pp. 116–18.

Figure 18 *Anne Seymour Damer* by Harriet Carr, 1788. National Galleries of Scotland. Transferred from the National Gallery of Scotland, 1950

He presents her as herself "in costume" with no reference to her role as an artist. Here she slides into the category of a fashionable aristocrat, dressed for her portrait; her skill as an actress is reflected in the fact that Reynolds wished to portray her as both a performer and a lady.

2.2 Attacks on the Artist As Actress and the Actress As Artist

As much as Georgian society flocked to private theatricals, the anxiety circulating around the potential power of female performers and the possible interchangeability between aristocrats and actresses is reflected in Damer's role as Lady Selina in Mary Berry's play *Fashionable Friends*. In the original performance of the play, Berry was Mrs. Lovell, the lovely sentimental heroine trapped in what she perceives to be an ordinary and unfulfilling marriage, and Damer played Lady Selina, a stylish, narcissistic aristocrat who cleverly plots her own freedom by convincing a doctor that because of her "nerves" she must be released from her domestic duties to travel to Naples. Offstage, Berry, Horace Walpole's ward, and Damer, Walpole's niece, were involved in a passionate relationship documented in part in the few handwritten notebooks of Damer's that still exist. While Berry's play is a comedy that makes fun of all things "fashionable" at the end of the century, reviving archetypal characters and plotlines from Restoration drama, the play contains a deep sense of irony. As Andrew Elfenbien has argued, audiences at Strawberry Hill would have enjoyed and understood the multiple layers of meaning attached to the "friendship" portrayed between Mrs. Lovell and Lady Selina because of the offstage bond between the actresses.[78]

In the first scene that we encounter Mrs. Lovell and Selina, they discuss Mrs. Lovell's portrait:

> Mrs. Lovell: Would heaven I were thus at liberty to follow every dictate of my heart! – but the being to whom fate has united me, seems to have lost all idea of the attentions, of the duties of minds of superior order. Would you believe he was out of patience with my sending an express after you, with my picture, the night you left me?
>
> Lady Selina Vapour: Abominable! When he knew that I had sent to the painters for it every two hours of the day before I left town, and was in despair of going without it?[79]

What is particularly interesting about this moment is the connection Berry makes between Mrs. Lovell's "real" self and her portable, circulating image captured in art. The joke here relies on the audience's understanding of the fashionable practice of exchanging portrait miniatures. These negotiations often symbolized the dynamics of friendship or personal attachment. For the actresses Berry and Damer, who are simultaneously artists and authors offstage, this reference to the self as commodity and to the practice of image-making underscores the multilayered meanings of the dramatic text as well as the practice of ghosting their real-life personas on stage. At the end of the play, everyone ends up with an appropriate partner, except for the fashionable Lady Selina, who is ostracized and on her own. Although it might be tempting to read this conclusion as a moral lesson about the dissipated virtues and bleak prospects for independent women, it can also be seen as a statement about the politics of female agency and the threat of the effects of the art of the actress – both on the stage and on canvas.

It is not surprising that satiric prints of Damer and Kauffman center on the figure of the female artist in her studio. Both artists had studios in their homes. As Angela Rosenthal reminds us:

---

[78] Elfenbien, "Lesbian Aestheticism," 10–11. See also Schmid, "Mary Berry's *Fashionable Friends* on Stage," 172–7.

[79] Berry, *Fashionable Friends*, Act II, Scene 1, pp. 18–19.

As a hybrid of public and private symbolic space, the portraitists' studio was designed to stage ideal relations both public and private. The portrait event afforded artist and sitter alike the opportunity to present themselves to each other in a space traversed by complex networks of visuality and sociability. On the one hand, the sitter performed an act of public presentation – to the artist, and, depending on the finished portrait's intended audience, to a broader public. On the other hand, the intimacy of pleasantries and exchanges meant that both artist and sitter were brought into a relation usually thought of as private ... The artist managed the space, often directing the performances that took place within it. The quasi-domestic, malleable space of the portrait studio offered artist, and especially female artists, an ideal space for the crafting of a virtuous artistic self.[80]

Kauffman, in particular, cultivated her career through the celebrated space of her studio designed to welcome patrons, friends, and celebrities. Princess Dashkova, who met Damer while traveling in Italy, describes Damer's studio as a semiprivate space, open only to a select group of friends:

The mornings we spent sightseeing and excursions which usually ended at Mrs. Damer's studio. For it was not in her boudoir that her friends found her – rather did they find her wrestling with a block of marble, trying to impart to it the shape she wanted. But it was a sanctum open only to her closest friends. She was very modest by nature and would never parade her talents and her learning.[81]

Dashkova's need to characterize Damer as modest, in a sentence after she provides an image of the artist "wrestling with a block of marble," suggests the threatening nature of Damer's artistic practice. The unsettling 1789 caricature *The Damerian Apollo* (Figure 19) is a scathing attack on Damer, who is depicted making a sculpture in her studio. Damer is placed in a lewd position using her chisel on the backside of a classical male sculpture. She is assisted by another woman with her back to the viewer, who holds up her hand to shield the statues' genitals, finding herself also in a lewd position. A 1772 caricature of Kauffman titled *The Paintress of Macaronis* similarly represents her in a studio space, sitting in front of her portraits of foppish men ("macaronis") with large wigs, holding two very long paintbrushes poised in phallic positions.[82] These images clearly illustrate that anxieties associated with female artists centered around performances and performance spaces. Questioning the propriety of women making art, these mockeries redirected the effects of artworks made by women to the theater of their creation. The satirists mount a direct attack on the

---

[80] A. Rosenthal, *Angelica Kauffman*, p. 83.
[81] Dashkova, *Memoirs of Princess Dashkova*, p. 175.
[82] This image, with a short descriptive essay by Baumgärtel, can be found at: www.angelika-kauffmann.de/en/gossip.

Figure 19 *The Damerian Apollo*, pub. by Wm Holland, July 1, 1789. Courtesy of the Lewis Walpole Library, Yale University

theatricality of Damer's and Kauffman's artistic practices and restage their studio spaces as obscene and ridiculous.

2.3 Cleopatra Scenes

Although their choices of scenes and composition are different, it is striking that Anne Damer and Angelica Kauffman both chose to represent Cleopatra, perhaps the most famous foreign queen and theatrical heroine, in the process of mourning with other women. Kauffman's *Cleopatra Adorning the Tomb of Mark Antony* (ca. 1769–70) portrays Cleopatra mourning her beloved Mark Antony surrounded by her female attendants Iras and Charmion.[83] The painting is evocative and haunting. The women form a circle over the casket – one holds a torch, the other a handful of flowers, while Cleopatra lays a wreath on the head of the tomb. In 1788, nearly twenty years later, Damer created a sculptural relief for Boydell's Shakespeare Gallery depicting Cleopatra at the end of

---

[83] The painting can be viewed online: https://collections.burghley.co.uk/collection/cleopatra-dec orating-the-tomb-of-mark-anthony-by-angelica-kauffmann-r-a-1741-1807/.

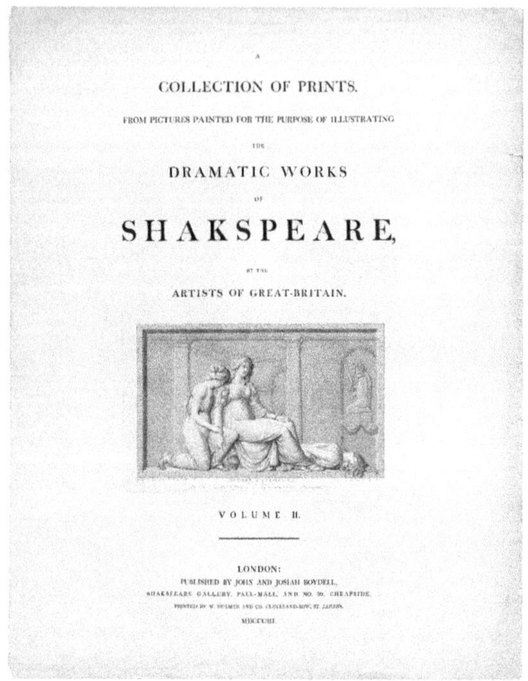

Figure 20 *Antony & Cleopatra* [graphic]: Modelled in basso relievo / by the Honble. A. S. Damer; engraved by Thos. Hellyer. Pub. June 4, 1803, by J. and J. Boydell, London. Courtesy of the Lewis Walpole Library, Yale University

Shakespeare's play just moments after Iras's suicide (Figure 20). Here, Charmion buries her head in Cleopatra's shoulder, anticipating her demise.[84]

Kauffman's and Damer's depictions of Cleopatra can be seen as shared narratives of female solidarity and emotion. For Angela Rosenthal, Kauffman's archiving of her portraits of women reimagines a space of female creativity outside of the boundaries of male artistic practice: "Kauffman kept small copies of her portraits of many of the famous women she painted. Keeping with her reminders of her relationships with these peers, Kauffman opened up a notional space of feminine creative exchange, an alternative realm beyond the often problematic, misogynist strictures of academic and public artistic practice."[85] Kauffman would continue to produce images of women grieving throughout her career. The frozen, timeless quality of Damer's representations of herself and her female muses through sculpture is similarly a commemoration of the dynamics of female artistry,

---

[84] See Barchas, "Reporting on What Jane Saw 2.0," for more about female artists and actresses and their relationship to Boydell's gallery.

[85] A. Rosenthal, *Angelica Kauffman*, p. 170.

friendship, collaboration, and loss. Damer's and Kaufman's attention to collective female performances, grief, and creativity offers strategies for memorializing their muses and themselves simultaneously. Through the shared practices of the artist and the actress they enact legacies of forgotten connection and archives of feeling.

Our access to Damer's and Kauffman's work today comes through our interactions with their artworks either via reproductions or the theater of the museum (and now, often, on the Internet). As spectators in the present, our analysis and appreciation of their works depends on our own dynamics of performance as well as our engagement with their creations. We can walk around Damer's busts at the Metropolitan Museum, then go upstairs to visit Kauffman's history paintings. We can see their self-portraits together in the same hallway in the Uffizi Gallery in Florence. In this sense we are "being and becoming" as well, in tandem with their representations of themselves and others, participating in the lasting effects of the art of the actress.

3 Mary Anne's Muff: Actresses and Satire

In 1809, dressed in a sumptuous light-blue gown and carrying a large white muff, Mary Anne Clarke, the mistress of the Duke of York (the king's second son and commander in chief of the armed forces), testified before Parliament that she had sold army commissions to the highest bidders to decorate the large mansion bequeathed to her by her royal lover (Figure 21). An unprecedented series of revelations followed that uncovered widespread corruption in Parliament and offices of the government. If Mary Anne Clarke, a high-class courtesan, had access to selling promotions, who else had bought their advancement, and what could be done about it? The scandal caused an outcry against the government that eventually led to the duke's resignation as commander of the army. Caught in an onslaught of negative publicity, captured in many satiric prints by well-known caricaturists such as Thomas Rowlandson and Isaac Cruikshank, Clarke attempted to defend herself by threatening to publish her memoirs featuring private love letters from the duke. The duke in turn tried to suppress the publication of the text. Clarke persevered, composing additional pamphlets and filing several lawsuits. She was subsequently convicted of libel for her narrative version of the events. Not surprisingly, Mary Anne Clarke's body, fashion choices, and theatricality feature prominently in representations of her that center on the nature of her feminine duplicity and dangerous sexuality. Clarke's attempts to portray herself as an innocent heroine are parodied through references to her role as a mistress, her desire for fame and luxury, and her connections to famous actresses such as Sarah Siddons and Dorothy Jordan, herself the longtime mistress of the Duke of Clarence.

Figure 21 *Mrs. M. A. Clarke* by Charles Williams, February 25, 1809. Courtesy of the Lewis Walpole Library, Yale University

The vexed case of Mary Anne Clarke highlights the relationship between actresses, politics, seduction, royalty, and caricature in the late eighteenth century.[86]

Born around 1776, in Chancery Lane, an urban neighborhood populated by solicitors, wigmakers, law-stationers, booksellers, and prostitutes, Mary Anne Clarke was exposed to the seedy underworld of print from a young age. Her father died when she was a child, and her mother remarried to a man who worked for a printer. Mary Anne apparently supplemented her family's income by copyediting and proofreading in the printing house, a process that involved reading the text out loud. She eloped with Joseph Clarke, an alcoholic gambler, in 1791 and had four children (one died in infancy). By 1800, she had acquired several rich admirers, one of whom introduced her to Frederick, the Duke of York, who provided her with a glamorous house in Gloucester Place, making no

---

[86] There are no full-length biographies of Mary Anne Clarke, who was also the great-grandmother of the novelist Daphne du Maurier. Du Maurier's novel *Mary Anne* (1954) is based on her dynamic relative. For two excellent articles, see Breashears, "Desperately Seeking Mary Anne Clarke"; Turner, "Daphne du Maurier's *Mary Anne*."

attempt to keep their liaison a secret from the public or his wife, Princess Frederica Charlotte of Prussia. In 1805, Joseph Clarke reappeared and threatened to sue the duke for adultery. This led the duke to break things off with Clarke and to take back his promise to pay her a meager annuity of 400 pounds a year. After a failed attempt to bribe him to buy back her letters, a tactic used successfully by the actress Mary Robinson after her disastrous affair with the Prince of Wales, Clarke moved out of her large house, sold many of her belongings, and eventually teamed up with Gwyllym Lloyd Wardle, a Member of Parliament and an opposition radical, who instigated the investigation of the duke in the House of Commons in January 1809.

The trial and its aftermath became a media sensation, producing countless caricatures, broadsides, pamphlets, and engravings. Rowlandson himself made 200 images relating to the Clarke scandal. While there is also a part two to this story involving the suppression, burning, and subsequent publication of several "authentic memoirs" and narrative versions of these events, which are analyzed in an excellent essay by Caroline Breashears, in this section, I will be focusing on a variety of images of Clarke, highlighting the connections between her notorious celebrity and specific actresses, plays, theatrical motifs, and fashionable accessories. While elsewhere I have argued that muffs in portraits of actresses were simultaneously symbols of luxury and sexuality, looking closely at representations of Clarke's muff in particular underscores the pervasive paradoxical ambiguity of women performing in the public sphere.[87] Like an actress, Mary Anne Clarke's skill was in her seductive, persuasive talents, an ability that allowed her to turn the government upside down. Mary Anne's white muff, a symbol of her wealth, status, and "purity," is itself a genius move of sartorial satire. Clarke was acutely aware of her visibility and the messages she could send with her outfit choices. The white muff, which she knew would be recorded and reported in the press, prints, and caricatures, was part of a branding strategy designed to build on her image as a desirable woman of fashion and integrity.[88] At the same time, it was a cheeky move, a kind of in-your-face, attention-seeking moment meant to absorb the spotlight. Which it did.

Why did the Mary Anne Clarke scandal invite such intense scrutiny and outrage? Primarily because the public was fascinated by Clarke's connection to the royals, who were themselves celebrities. The Duke of York was just one royal family member who was embroiled in scandal. Some of these other notorious activities included the Prince of Wales and his lovers, particularly his past liaisons and negotiations with the actress and author Mary Robinson;

---

[87] See Engel, *Austen, Actresses, and Accessories*; Engel, "Muff Affair."

[88] For more about muffs, see Hillary Davidson, *Dress in the Age of Jane Austen*; Batchelor and Larkin, *Jane Austen Embroidery*; Engel, *Austen, Actresses, and Accessories*.

the king's madness; early investigations of Princess Caroline and her possible amours in "the delicate investigation"[89]; and the most obvious parallel with Clarke, the celebrated actress Dorothy Jordan, who became mistress to the Duke of Clarence and mother to ten of his children. According to Claire Tomalin, Jordan's most recent biographer, 1809 (the height of the Mary Anne Clarke scandal) was a year of disasters for Jordan. A fire destroyed part of St James's Palace in January, prompting her to ask the Duke of Clarence if she and their children could move out of their rooms and be settled in a house in town. A month later, a horrific fire destroyed the new Drury Lane Theatre – all her costumes were burnt and other priceless items were lost. Between these events, the Mary Anne Clarke debacle "set the press off in full cry against the royal brothers."[90] Tomalin speculates about the reasons the Duke of Clarence might have had for insisting that Jordan abandon her theatrical career. She writes:

> His dignity took precedence over her convenience and career; very possibly he was thinking of the dignity of the children also. If Dora could be made less conspicuous, the children might seem less like her children and more like his; rather than there being any question of their moving out of St. James's Palace, they might more easily take their place within the royal family.[91]

The duke's concerns illustrate the scope of circulating anxieties about the visibility of women as professionals and performers in relation to the reputation of the royal family.[92] Although Clarke was not an actress on the stage, her theatrical maneuvering and publicity stunts established her as a performer to be reckoned with.

It's not surprising, then, that Rowlandson would craft an image of Mary Anne Clarke in his series of caricatures chronicling the scandal that looks just like Dorothy Jordan. This mirroring underscores the potential threat of female power, presence, and manipulation, as well as the ways in which performances can lead to damaging modes of trespassing and infiltration. These parallels also provide information about the visual literacy of audiences – in other words, how spectators understood identities through theatrical cues and signifiers associated with fashion, costume, gesture, and iconography drawn from other art forms, particularly the theater and portraiture. Here I am echoing what David Francis Taylor, Amelia Rauser, Cindy McCreery, and Heather McPherson have eloquently argued about caricature as an intermedial art form and the ways in which images are intended to be read on multiple levels.[93] Ultimately, looking

---

[89] See Fraser, *Unruly Queen*, p. 233.   [90] Tomalin, *Mrs Jordan's Profession*, p. 208.

[91] Tomalin, *Mrs Jordan's Profession*, p. 210.

[92] For more on Jordan's career and family life, see Phillips, *Carrying All before Her*; Perry, *Spectacular Flirtations*.

[93] Compare Taylor, *Politics of Parody*; Rauser, *Caricature Unmasked*; MacPherson, *Art and Celebrity*, particularly pages 127–56; McCreery, *Satirical Gaze*.

closely at the following images, I am exploring Mary Anne Clarke's art in orchestrating and performing this drama, the art and politics of fashioning her own image, and the critical response to her self-fashioning in caricatures, prints, and other materials. I'm also interested in the potential resonance of Clarke's talking back to the establishment, her ambition for self and family, her exposure of oppressive patriarchal structures, and her desire to have the last word.

3.1 Glamour Girl

Regency portrait painter Adam Buck completed a painting of Mary Anne Clarke in 1803 as a fashionable society hostess (Figure 22), several years before she was at the center of the government scandal that caused a media sensation. Posed next to the base of a statue, Clarke is elegantly dressed as a stylish and virtuous neoclassical figure. The artist associates her image with timeless,

Figure 22 *Portrait of a Lady,* from a drawing by Adam Buck (*Mary Anne Clarke at the Base of a Statue*), 1803. From *The Connoisseur,* vol. XLI (1915). Lewis Walpole Library, Yale University

idealized beauty. Additional images of Clarke as a glamorous heroine borrow from classical motifs and iconography. In a print made by Buck, with an inscription that reads "drawn from life," Clarke is seated on a couch in a diaphanous gown with her legs crossed. The viewer's eye is drawn to the folds of her gown, which are elegant as well as sexually suggestive. In another image, Clarke is shown in profile, mimicking an ancient marble bust. Her gown falls off her shoulders, and she wears a headband with a classical pattern.[94] The caption on the former stating "drawn from life" and Clarke's signature on the latter suggest that these are pictures that Clarke approved of and posed for, establishing her own investment in her sartorial presence and the production of her image.

Recently, a curious watercolor of Clarke by Buck appeared in an auction catalogue (Figure 23).[95] The image depicts Clarke in her characteristic elegant white gown, with her hand suggestively on her hip and the hem of her skirt lifted to reveal her ankles. She looks directly at the viewer with an expression of mild annoyance. Placed alongside Buck's original image of Clarke, represented as a graceful statue, this picture seems to function as a kind of outtake or "B-roll" snapshot of Clarke stepping out of the expected pose and frame. The look on her face suggests that she wishes to be in control of the scene; she dares the spectator to look at her and take her seriously. We can never know if this is the way Clarke actually appeared to Buck, or if he created this picture to tell a story about Clarke's stubbornness and performativity. Either way, it is a startling glimpse at Clarke's persona – real or imagined.

In her brilliant work on the significance of neoclassical dress for women in the Regency period, Amelia Rauser points out the fine line between fashion and embodied suggestion in the style and drape of neoclassical garments.[96] Although these portraits may have been designed to promote Clarke's identity as a respectable society beauty, the images simultaneously advertised the availability of her body. This duality made it easy for artists like Rowlandson to satirize Clarke by highlighting her clothing, the staging and placement of her body, and her accessories. Caricatures of Clarke offer a visual argument for the inherent contradiction of women who are perpetually on display. Do women who participate in styling, curating, and performing their self-images (something that was very necessary to sustain celebrity status) gain agency from this process? Or is their participation in their own commodification an act of

---

[94] This latter drawing can be viewed online: www.sciencephoto.com/media/553168/view/mary-anne-clarke.

[95] See the Jarndyce catalogue, List 3: www.jarndyce.co.uk/catalogues/pdfs/ORIGINAL_ARTWORK_PRINTS_E-LIST_3.pdf.

[96] Rauser, *Age of Undress*, pp. 22–8.

Figure 23 *Portrait of Mary Anne Clarke* by Adam Buck, 1804. Lewis Walpole Library, Yale University

submission and objectification? Clarke's approval of the "legitimate" images of her is shadowed by the sheer number of satiric prints that emphasize the dangerous, immoral, and excessive quality of her performances.

A portrait titled *Mrs. Clarke the York Magnet* by an unknown artist (Figure 24), printed during 1809, the year the scandal took place, borrows from the details of earlier images – Clarke in a neoclassical gown lying on a couch – and underscores the idea of Clarke as her own "brand." She is a "magnet" for a wealthy lover, scandal, fame, and infamy. The artist here seems to suggest that Clarke's self-fashioning has been extremely effective. Also published in 1809, the caricature *A Sleeping Partner in a Late York Commission Warehouse. Dreaming of Mischief*, by Charles Williams, depicts a sleeping Clarke stretched out on a striped couch under a dramatic red curtain,

Figure 24 *Mrs. Clarke the York Magnet,* by unknown artist, published 1809. National Portrait Gallery

surrounded by evidence of her letters of corruption.[97] The image references the fashion plates already shown, but also echoes well-known portraits of reclining female figures, Venus in particular. Representing Clarke as a corrupted Venus, Williams emphasizes the consequences of her seductive performances.

3.2 Mary Anne Clarke and Dorothy Jordan

Perhaps the most impressive visual tribute to the wide-ranging significance of the Mary Anne Clarke scandal is Thomas Rowlandson's *Complete Collection of Caricatures Relative to Mrs. Clarke,* published by Thomas Teggs in 1809. Rowlandson's group of prints resemble a serial novel, or multiple scenes from a play, and are scattered through the digital realm.[98] For the contemporary researcher, encountering them image by image is a different experience than owning the entire collection. The title page is framed like an opening act in

---

[97] This image can be viewed online: https://worcester.emuseum.com/objects/41935/a-sleeping-partner-in-a-late-york-commission-warehouse-dr.

[98] The title-page illustration may be viewed here: www.metmuseum.org/art/collection/search/392762. The British Museum and the Lewis Walpole Library Digital Collections have many of the other images.

Figure 25 *Dorothy Jordan* by James Heath, after John Russell, 1802. National Portrait Gallery

a theater; Clarke's dress, collar, necklace, and hairstyle mimic a well-known portrait of Dorothy Jordan by John Russell in 1802 (Figure 25). Connecting Clarke's image to the celebrated actress Jordan, who was well-known for her royal liaison, brings Clarke into the murky world of the female professional performer. Jordan's ability to snag a royal partner through her theatrical success is aligned with Clarke's failed attempt to garner economic security and social standing from his brother, the Duke of York. Rowlandson returns to motifs of the theater and performance throughout the caricatures to highlight Clarke's association with acting and theatricality.

In Rowlandson's *The Road to Preferment through Clarkes Passage*, published March 5, 1809 (Figure 26), the artist places Clarke's figure on a stage at the entrance to a "passage" or tunnel, creating an obscene reference to the entrance to Clarke's own body. The platform is besieged by an army of men,

Figure 26 Thomas Rowlandson, *The Road to Preferment through Clarkes Passage*, etching with hand-coloring, published March 5, 1809, by Thomas Tegg. Lewis Walpole Library, Yale University

some in military garb, rushing toward her in an effort to get her attention. Clarke dons a military jacket and hat, an image that resembles John Hoppner's painting of Dorothy Jordan as Hypolita in Colley Cibber's *She Would and She Would Not* (Figure 27). Claire Tomalin points out that Jordan became known for her cross-dressed roles, particularly her military parts and her impersonation of young men with swords.[99] Clarke is similarly depicted with military accessories, echoing her connection to Jordan and the actress's enticing performances of masculinity. On Rowlandson's stage, Clarke declares theatrically: "Gentlemen it is no use to rush on in this manner – the principal places have been disposed of these three weeks and I assure you at present there is not even standing room." Employing the language of the theater – "principal places" instead of "principal parts," and only "standing room" – Rowlandson underscores Clarke's connection to the figure of the sexualized actress whose business is to publicly sell her body/parts. The details of Clarke's costumes in these prints highlight the dueling iconography of satire and legitimacy in depictions of actresses.

Rowlandson also associated Clarke with women's roles in popular eighteenth-century plays. In his *Dissolution of Partnership, or the Industrious*

---

[99] Tomalin, *Mrs Jordan's Profession*, pp. 72, 113.

Figure 27 *Dorothy Jordan* by John Hoppner, 1791. National Portrait Gallery

Mrs. Clarke Winding up Her Accounts, published February 15, 1809, by Thomas Tegg, Rowlandson portrays Clarke receiving a money bag from a large man acting as a mediator between her and an emaciated army officer (Figure 28). Behind her, a parted curtain reveals an oval portrait of her lover, the Duke of York, above a list of names of those "offered" promotions. A quote from Jonathan Gay's famous satiric play aimed at the corruption of mid-century London, *The Beggar's Opera*, hangs above the duke's head: "Tis Woman that seduces all mankind / By her we first are taught the wheedling arts / Her very eyes can cheat when most she's kind / She tricks us of our mon[e]y with our hearts." Rowlandson thus connects Clarke's role in the commission scandal with the theatricality and deception of the actress. Her private and public "performances" have "exposed" the immorality and depravity of her true character.

In Rowlandson's *More of the Clarke, or Fresh Accusations*, published July 14, 1809, by Thomas Tegg, Clarke stands dramatically posed in front of a dressing table, mirror, and bed partially hidden behind curtains (Figure 29). The Duke of York has his back to Clarke and faces a jeering audience. Clarke compares the duke to Felix, a biblical character who rose from slavery to become a corrupt governor. She proclaims, "Thou art the Man – behold the Furniture!" – a satiric reference to the lavish home decorations Clarke funded with the bribe money she received for army commissions. The Duke of York

Figure 28 Thomas Rowlandson, *Dissolution of Partnership, or the Industrious Mrs. Clarke Winding up Her Accounts*, etching with hand-coloring, published February 15, 1809, by Thomas Tegg. Lewis Walpole Library, Yale University

Figure 29 Thomas Rowlandson, *More of the Clarke, or Fresh Accusations*, etching and stipple with hand-coloring, published July 14, 1809, by Thomas Tegg. Lewis Walpole Library, Yale University

retorts that "it was all for the good of my Country. I assure you I am as firm a patriot as ever purchased a convex Mirror, or a red turkey Carpet." Rowlandson places the two characters onstage to emphasize the depth of their morally suspect exchanges. Clarke's blue empire-waist dress echoes images of the dress she wore for her first appearance before the House of Commons. Here Rowlandson may also be taking the opportunity to align the Duke of York with unflattering images of the famous actor John Phillip Kemble. The duke's exaggerated nose echoes caricatures of Kemble that highlight this prominent feature.[100]

3.3 Mary Anne's Muff(s)

In addition to Rowlandson's conflation of Clarke's image with Jordan's, in several of his compositions he took inspiration from Clarke's well-publicized outfit from her first day of testimony in the House of Commons. For Rowlandson and other artists, Clarke's blue coat, veil, and large white muff became signature elements of her visual identity. Her muff, a sexually inviting and charged accessory that can also paradoxically signify wealth and status, appears in a variety of sizes and colors in satiric prints depicting Clarke in a range of situations. Although we can't ever be certain of the original coloring of eighteenth- and early nineteenth-century prints, as colors vary and may have faded over time, it is safe to say that in some images Clarke's muff appears lighter than in others. In a version of Rowlandson's titled *The York March*, published by Thomas Tegg in 1809, for example, Clarke's muff looks very brown. The description of a print of this image at the Boston Public Library reads as follows:

> The stout Duke of York has turned his sturdy back on his fair enslaver, declaring, "If I must march, I must; however, I shall leave my Baggage behind me!" The principal cause of the exposure may be laid to the Duke's account. He declined . . . to keep his word in respect to an allowance of four hundred a year, which, there appears no doubt, he had promised to make the lady, if her conduct, after his desertion, was such as to merit his approval. Mrs. Clarke, who is dressed precisely as she appeared at the bar of the House of Commons, is thus reproaching the York deserter. The storm which was raised during the enquiry into the abuses of privilege in the administration of the army and Half-Pay Fund, and threatened to deprive the Duke of his office

---

[100] Gillray's caricature *Theatrical Mendicants Relieved*, January 1809, depicts Siddons and Kemble begging for money from the Duke of Cumberland after the devastating Covent Garden fire. Siddons and Kemble have pronounced noses, emphasizing their "greedy" Jewishness and efforts at self-promotion. See https://branchcollective.org/?ps_articles=terry-f-robinson-national-theatre-in-transition-the-london-patent-theatre-fires-of-1808-1809-and-the-old-price-riots.

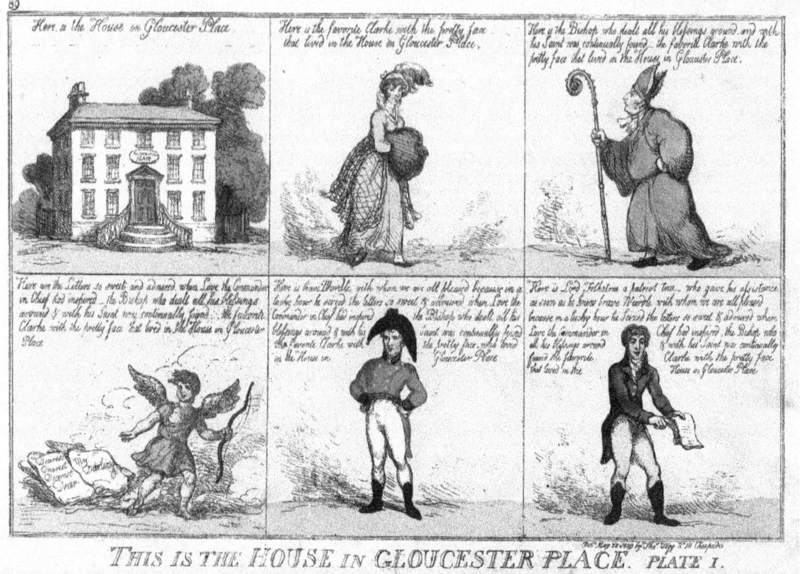

Figure 30 Thomas Rowlandson, *This Is the House in Gloucester Place*, etching and stipple with hand-coloring, published May 28, 1809, by Thomas Tegg. Lewis Walpole Library, Yale University

> as Commander-in-Chief, only hardened his resolution to do nothing for this Ariadne, who, however, to do her justice, showed herself well able to defend her own interests, and to pay back her defamers in their own coin.[101]

Here Rowlandson connects the duke's reference to Clarke as "baggage" to the unwieldy furry accessory. Clarke's brown muff can be seen as a sexualized, denigrating signifier. Her defense, that she has been deceived and will be left without protection, is undercut by the brown object.

Clarke's brown muff appears again in Rowlandson's *This Is the House in Gloucester Place*, May 26, 1809 (Figure 30). The repeated refrain "the favorite Clarke with the pretty face, that lived in the house on Gloucester Place," ties this caricature to popular broadsides that related the story of the scandal in verse that people could memorize and participate in reciting.[102] Rowlandson's repetition of the brown muff over several images converts the accessory into a signification of his idea of Clarke. Rowlandson's serial images and narratives

---

[101] The image can be viewed online: www.digitalcommonwealth.org/search/commonwealth:tq57ph60r.

[102] For more on muff caricatures and the connections between muffs and representations of actresses, see Engel, *Austen, Actresses, and Accessories*.

of Clarke highlight the importance of reading the caricatures separately and together as a fascinating intertextual web.

In an even more elaborate 1809 print, *The York Sparring Match, Being M. A. Clarke's First Set to, & Who Is Likely to Become the Champion of All England* by S. W. Fores, Clarke is involved in a full-on battle with members of the trial, military officers, and the public.[103] The scene is a theatrical spectacle with an audience watching Clarke as she attempts to defend her honor with a sword – a typical role for a man or male actor. Wielding her weapon, she is able to "cut off" the body parts of a number of men, who react accordingly – for example, "I am struck dumb, and lost my thumb!"; "Oh! Dear! Oh dear! She has cut off my ear"; "Take her into custody, she will be too much for us – send her to York Jail." In this image, a white muff is detached from Clarke's body and takes on a life of its own as a discarded thing next to a pile of love letters. Here the accessory becomes an example of corrupted, potentially dangerous, but ultimately ineffective weaponry. Clarke's castrating blade causes the duke to accuse her of being "too much for us." Fores's image captures several threads of anxiety circulating around Clarke's performances. As a woman who has called for a trial and is providing testimony that might alter the working of the government and the reputation of the royal family, she is assuming masculine prerogative and overstepping her role. Furthermore, if you provide such a female with a sword (metaphorical agency) then as a man you risk being literally and figuratively cut down. The muff alone on the ground becomes an anthropomorphic sign for Clarke herself. Left to her own devices she becomes an excessive example of a female body part, and her acting spins out of control.

3.4 Aftermaths: Mary Anne Clarke and the Gallery of Beauties

Despite Mary Anne Clarke's attempts to rescue her public persona, she remained a figure of suspicion and ridicule. A fascinating image of an enormous King George III staring at a portrait of Clarke with a spyglass titled *The Connoisseur Viewing a Picture* (1810), by William Heath, suggests that the scandal of 1809 had wider resonance.[104] Clearly, the print is referencing and satirizing a culture of connoisseurship or artistic expertise that focuses on female bodies.[105] Clarke looks like a combination of images of royal mistresses of the past (Lely's Windsor Beauties, for example) as well as portraits of nude classical female figures. The configuration of the room as a portrait gallery

---

[103] *The York Sparring Match* can be seen online: www.britishmuseum.org/collection/object/ P_1868-0808-7740.

[104] Heath's *The Connoisseur Viewing a Picture* can be seen online: www.britishmuseum.org/ collection/object/P_1868-0808-6258.

[105] For more on portraits and connoisseurship, see Mudge, "Gazing Games."

suggests that Mary Anne Clarke epitomizes a past that haunts the present. The king's scrutiny also implies that as much as he tries to look, he cannot actually see what is right in front of him. The use of a spyglass in the composition ties the scene back to the dynamics of the theatre. The naked Clarke, trapped in a frame, passively gazing at the spectator, is unable to speak or claim an alternative form of agency, except for the fact that the king in his own grotesque embodiment seems to be looking past her. His figure is surrounded by portraits of nude women closing in on his throne. Heath may be proposing that the memory and lasting impact of seductive women (read: actresses Nell Gwyn, Dorothy Jordan, Mary Anne Clarke) on the royal family has caused a myopic breakdown of values and legitimacy.

After the scandal, Clarke commissioned a sculpture of herself as Clytie, a classical heroine turned into a sunflower, who is able to see all, but is trapped in one position (Figure 31). According to the National Portrait Gallery,

> Gahagan's bust was commissioned by Clarke herself and it is believed to have stood in her house between portraits of the Duke of York and Colonel Wardle. The pose, rising from the petals of a sunflower, may have been chosen as an allegory of the cast-off mistress. It derives from a celebrated Roman bust, part of the Towneley collection displayed at the British Museum from 1808, and

Figure 31 *Mary Anne Clarke*, by Lawrence Gahagan, 1811. National Portrait Gallery

then thought to represent Clytie, the deserted lover of Helios, who was changed into a sunflower so that she could follow her lover's progress across the sky each day.[106]

Clarke's depiction of herself as a figure of lasting beauty and grace is also tragically ironic. Things did not end well for her. Eventually she was imprisoned, and she never recovered her former glory. This sculpture, however, provides us with evidence of her embodied presence and her participation in creating and making her own image, an important counter to the satiric portraits that have since defined her. Tying Clarke's legacy to the art of the actress allows us to contextualize her strategies for self-fashioning and promotion as part of a larger series of methods used to shape the careers of female performers. In turn, satirists attacked her in the same way they leveled critiques at the leading actresses of the day. Clarke's beauty and cleverness, her ability to seduce and deceive along with her will to survive, made her the perfect analogy to the actress and/or to the woman who would stop at nothing to achieve her own goals.

4 Epilogue: Unfinished Business: Elizabeth Inchbald, Lady Cahir, Sir Thomas Lawrence, and the Aftermath of the Art of the Actress

In 1795, the actress, playwright, and novelist Elizabeth Inchbald sat for Thomas Lawrence in his Greek Street studio for a now well-known unfinished portrait that currently resides in a private collection (Figure 32). Lawrence's haunting image of Inchbald's luminous face emerging from a mysterious abstract background has often been compared to his unfinished triple portrait of *Emilia, Lady Cahir, Later Countess of Glengall*, composed between 1803 and 1805.[107] This extraordinary painting, inspired by Lady Cahir's performance in the private theatricals at Bentley Priory (1803), features three distinct views of the amateur actress, who dazzled audiences with her portrayal of Lady Contest in Inchbald's play *The Wedding Day* (1794) opposite Lawrence himself as the dashing Lord Rakeland.[108] Considering Lawrence's work in the context of the theatrical and artistic performances simultaneously occurring both on- and offstage provides further insight into the tangible and intangible effects of the art of the actress.

We don't know much about Lawrence's portrait of Inchbald, other than the fact that he began working on it soon after he met her through their mutual

---

[106] "Mary Anne Clarke (née Thompson)," *National Portrait Gallery*: www.npg.org.uk/collections/search/portrait/mw01323/Mary-Anne-Clarke-ne-Thompson.

[107] Though the rights to reproducing this image are restricted, it can be viewed online at the website of the Metropolitan Museum of Art: www.metmuseum.org/art/collection/search/656471.

[108] For an excellent catalogue and discussion of Thomas Lawrence's portraits, see Albinson, Funnel, and Peltz, eds., *Thomas Lawrence*.

Figure 32 *Mrs. Joseph Inchbald*, by Thomas Lawrence, ca. 1796. Private Collection Photo © Agnew's, London/Bridgeman Images

connections to the actress Sarah Siddons and her circle. The portrait was one of a number of unfinished paintings Lawrence exhibited in his studio, "to which the eye might be attracted as the mirrors of either, rank, beauty, or genius."[109] We have only a bit more knowledge of Lawrence's fascinating tripartite painting of Lady Cahir. The image has received quite a bit of attention from Lawrence scholars and enthusiasts, and it was among the paintings recovered from Lawrence's studio after his death. Lady Cahir tried to purchase it but did not succeed. According to one description of the blockbuster 2010 exhibit *Thomas Lawrence: Regency Power and Brilliance*, Lawrence's incomplete works "represented the liveliness, sense of spontaneity, and even sketchiness that Lawrence hoped to preserve in his finished portraits."[110] In other words, these paintings convey a sense of the embodied living presence of individuals at specific moments of time. Invoking the process of making and becoming, these portraits tell playful and poignant stories about the materialization of identities and the lasting effects of the art of the actress.

Looking closely at the many connections between these images, I would like consider the following questions: What is the multifaceted significance of the unfinished presentation of these portraits? What aspects of Lady Cahir's portrayal of Inchbald's heroine Lady Contest might be displayed in Lawrence's

---

[109] Albinson, "New Ambition," p. 193.	[110] Ibid.

dynamic fragments/close-ups of her image? How does Lawrence's representation of his artistic process mirror the dynamics of performance and memory? How do Lawrence's representations of Inchbald and Lady Cahir differ from other portraits of women he completed during this period – particularly his theatrical image of Sally Siddons (1795) (which he may have been working on while painting Inchbald's portrait, as well as his masterpiece *Isabella Wolff*, a project he began in 1803 and finished in 1815)? I propose that focusing on unfinished portrayals of Inchbald and Lady Cahir as subjects, models, and muses for Lawrence provides new ways of thinking about the afterlives of actresses in performance and the powerful representational strategies of female playwrights.

4.1 Portraits in Process

The genre of unfinished artworks can be traced back to the Renaissance, where the term "non-finito" was used to describe works by Titian, Michelangelo, and others who deliberately left parts of their works incomplete. A brilliant exhibit at the Metropolitan Museum titled *Unfinished: Thoughts Left Visible* (2016) collected a variety of works from the past and present to explore the idea of the unfinished across time periods and artistic genres. For the curators, Kelly Baum, Andrea Bayer, and Sheena Wagstaff, many artists, "Especially at the beginning of the nineteenth century, appear to have 'unfinished' the paintings and sculpture they produced. In so doing, they elided the acts of making and unmaking and confused the distinction between finished and unfinished."[111] Certainly, some works are unfinished because of the sudden death of the artist, but when an artist makes a deliberate choice to leave a work undone, this aesthetic strategy "designates works that seem to be unsettled, uncertain, provisional, unresolved, and open to change generally with regard to their style or process . . . Above all, seemingly unfinished works of art demand the active engagement of the viewer's imagination."[112] In turn, bringing this approach of active engagement to Lawrence's unfinished works reveals much about conceptions of the actress in the nineteenth century and their ongoing resonances today.

Lawrence's unfinished portraits are inextricably tied to the theater, an art form that is by definition fleeting, ephemeral, and open-ended, in that no performance can ever truly be the same thing twice. In an age before photography and video, theatrical performances left behind few tangible traces other than fragments of memory that might be conveyed or recorded by the actors or audience members, as well as visual materials and ephemera (portraits,

---

[111] Baum, Bayer, and Wagstaff, eds., *Unfinished*, p. 13.
[112] Baum, Bayer, and Wagstaff, eds., *Unfinished*, p. 14.

playbills, drawings, costume, set designs, promptbooks, etc.). Lawrence may have used the technique of the unfinished portrait as a way of translating his own flashes of memory – in other words, the mysterious ways in which Elizabeth Inchbald and Lady Cahir may have lingered theatrically in his imagination. Lawrence's portrait of Lady Cahir contains three distinct views of the sitter in different modes of completion – a drawing in graphite on the left (which is the way that Lawrence began all of his paintings, though difficult to see in the reproduction), a complete head study on the right, and in the center a partial view of the sitter in profile, an outline of her dress and back visible to the viewer. In both fully realized images, Lady Cahir looks directly at the viewer and the artist, staring seductively through the fourth wall of the canvas. The composition is surprisingly modern and cinematic; the blank unfinished space reflects what we can never see in paintings – the actual scene itself – yet the pieces of the portrait provide an uncanny sense of access to the process of making the painting and to the subject who performs in the scene. These unfinished compositions echo the dynamics of theatrical rehearsals. As rehearsal pieces, the paintings highlight the importance of possibilities, attempts, mistakes, revisions, and reworkings. They leave open a unique potential for desire and disruption. As Cassandra Albinson, a coeditor of the *Thomas Lawrence: Regency Power and Brilliance* exhibition catalogue, has observed, there is an unsettling intimacy of Lawrence's portraits of women. The Lady Cahir painting in particular seems to convey a specific fascination with her allure, as Lawrence wrote on the back of the portrait, "Painted by Thomas Lawrence in a fit of folly."[113] Lawrence's use of the word "folly," then, might allude to both his own sentiments and his consciousness of the processual approach to this work.

Lawrence's unfinished image of Inchbald conveys a different sense of intimacy but contains similar elements as in his triple image of Lady Cahir. Inchbald's head is fully rendered, her red hair appearing beneath a white cap and white neckline of a dress. The rest of her body is incomplete. Graphite lines sketch the contours of her clothing. She looks out languidly at the viewer with a calm, veiled expression. Lawrence portrays Inchbald as beautiful and mysterious. We have no idea what she might be thinking or what she might be capable of creating. I'd like to imagine that the effects of Lady Cahir's performance as Lady Contest in Inchbald's short provocative piece *The Wedding Day* in the Bentley Priory private theatricals left unfinished business. And indeed it may be this dynamic sense of the incomplete qualities of desire and longing that ties these portraits together. I am not suggesting that Lawrence was thinking directly about his portrait of Inchbald while painting Lady Cahir, but that

---

[113] Albinson, "New Ambition," p. 195.

Inchbald's presence is a part of Lawrence's composition inspired by Lady Cahir's performance of Inchbald's seductive and subversive heroine. The incompleteness of both portraits signals Lawrence's desire to keep the images in process, with figures perpetually coming into view. For the contemporary spectator, these portraits are alive because they are not done yet.

4.2 Private Theatricals

Inchbald's connection to private theatricals, intimacy, seduction, dangerous role-playing, and female agency is well known through Jane Austen's use of Inchbald's *Lovers' Vows* (1798) as the perfect plot vehicle for revealing the characters' erotic entanglements in *Mansfield Park* (1814). Elaine McGirr explores these ideas in her essay about the blurred lines between on- and offstage negotiations around a restaging of *Lovers' Vows* and parts of *Mansfield Park* that she directed at Chawton House in 2016.[114] Apparently, the performance brought out the best and worst in her young actors, who struggled to separate and channel their real-life insecurities and desires with the characters they were playing. The performance at Bentley Priory would have engendered similarly heightened emotions and blurred boundaries.

Most of what we know about the Bentley Priory private theatricals comes from the theater historian Sybil Rosenfeld. The first set of performances occurred on January 21, 1803, featuring two pieces by female playwrights, Inchbald's *The Wedding Day* and Hannah Cowley's *Who's the Dupe*. Lawrence participated in the performances and wrote about the decision to put on the theatricals in a letter to his sister:

> It was projected by a woman of great cleverness and beauty, Lady Cahir – very young and full of talent, with Lady Abercorn and the rest of the female party; and of course it was acceded to be Lord Abercorn, who, whatever character of pride the world may have given him, is just as pleasant and kind and gentlemanly with his family and friends as a man can be. It was determined to do it in a quiet way, and more as an odd experiment of the talents of the party than anything else; – but this and that friend would be offended; and at last it swelled up to a perfect theatre (in a room) and a London audience.[115]

He goes on to describe his involvement in the production:

> A terrifying bell rang, the curtain drew up, and the Wedding Day began. At first, I will own to you, Sheridan's face, the grave Duke of Devonshire, and two or three staunch critics, made one feel unpleasantly, for I opened the piece. However, this soon wore off. Our set all played extremely well – like

---

[114] McGirr, "Touching Scenes," pp. 164–72.
[115] Quoted in Rosenfeld, *Temples of Thespis*, p. 154.

persons of good sense without extravagance or buffoonery and yet with sufficient spirit. Lady Cahir, Mr. J. Maddox, and G. Lamb were the most conspicuous – the first so beautiful that I felt love-making very easy.[116]

What was it about Inchbald's play that brought out the best in Lady Cahir's performances and perhaps inspired Lawrence's portrait? *The Wedding Day* is a short two-act play that centers on the possibilities of romance and seduction within the confines of marital conventions and societal expectations. The play begins with the youthful, lovely Lady Contest marrying an older, sentimental Sir Adam Contest who has lost his first wife at sea. Lady Contest meets the dashing Rakeland and sparks fly in a witty scene where they trade lines in rapid succession and declare their impossible love for one another. Ultimately, in a bizarre twist of fate, it turns out that Sir Contest's beloved first wife has not drowned and her appearance in the second act releases Lady Contest from her obligations to her geriatric spouse. Inchbald wrote *The Wedding Day* specifically for the comedic actress and singer Dorothy Jordan, and it is clearly designed with her talents in mind. But there was something about the mix of the play, Lady Cahir's beauty, her acting talents, and the circumstances of the performance that captivated Lawrence to such a degree that he became swept up in "a fit of folly." Lady Cahir, a married Irish aristocrat and socialite, represented an impossible partner for Lawrence. This is of course the main danger and anxiety associated with private theatricals – that those who take part in them might forget their roles offstage in favor of their theatrical parts.

4.3 Passionate Portrayals

Lawrence himself had a long history of romantic entanglements with available and unavailable women. It's interesting to note that the same year he began Elizabeth Inchbald's portrait, he also completed a portrait of Sarah Siddons's daughter Sally, and left uncompleted one of another daughter, Maria (Figure 33).[117] Elsewhere I have written about Lawrence's involvement with both of Siddons's daughters, Sally and Maria, and the aftereffects of those doomed affairs.[118] In his paintings, he uses very different strategies and techniques to portray Sally and Maria. Sally's portrait is fully complete, theatrical, posed, and a bit over the top; Maria's is incomplete, haunting, wild, and unsettling. Lawrence may have drawn inspiration for Sally's portrait from his

---

116 Rosenfeld, *Temples of Thespis*, p. 155.

117 This Lawrence portrait of Sally Siddons can be viewed online: https://commons.wikimedia.org/wiki/File:Sally_Siddons_by_Thomas_Lawrence.jpg.

118 Engel, *Women, Performance, and the Material of Memory*, pp. 53–80.

Figure 33 *Maria Siddons*, print by George Clint after Sir Thomas Lawrence, between 1800 and 1830. Yale Center for British Art, Paul Mellon Collection

earlier painting of the actress, performer, and renowned beauty Emma Hamilton – the expression, pose and composition are similar.[119]

In 1803, when Lawrence began his portrait of Lady Cahir, he also embarked on a composition that would take him thirteen years to complete, his dazzling painting of Isabella Wolff (Figure 34), which I have argued contains elements of Lawrence's image of Sally Siddons (for example, note the erotically suggestive elbow).[120] Wolff is posed as a statue, echoing casts and miniatures of actual classical artworks. Her figure may have been modeled after one of Michelangelo's Sybils. The composition is a blend of classical and modern elements with extraordinary attention to accessories and details. Isabella Wolff was one of Lawrence's great passions – someone who admired art and considered herself an intellectual connoisseur. She is depicted in deep contemplation with a book of images of antique sculpture. Unlike his unfinished paintings of Inchbald and Lady Cahir, Lawrence labored obsessively over Wolff's portrait, suggesting his anxiety and

---

[119] On Lawrence's portrait of Emma Hamilton, see Funnell, "Lawrence among Men," pp. 2–3.

[120] Engel, *Women, Performance, and the Material of Memory*, p. 64. See also Albinson, "New Ambition," pp. 212–15; Albinson, "Construction of Desire, Lawrence's Portraits of Women," pp. 27–54.

Figure 34 *Isabella Wolff*, by Sir Thomas Lawrence, 1803–15.
Art Institute of Chicago

perfectionism. The painting is almost *too* finished. The differences between these strategies may reflect Lawrence's attitudes toward his sitters, but it also suggests the range of techniques of portrayal available to him as well as the diverse modalities he used to celebrate various subjects and artistic genres in his works.

In a recent article about the significance of Inchbald's *Remarks for the British Theatre*, Lisa Freeman argues brilliantly that Inchbald's genius in particular came from her purchase on the dramatic probabilities necessary for successful performances. She explains:

> In Inchbald's account, all successful dramatic stagings ought to be understood as lively collaborations between the skills of the playwright and the creative gifts of the actor ... Wielding both foresight and wisdom, skilled playwrights arrange their works for the "purpose of exhibition," that is, they provide the bold scaffolding and framework within which adept actors and actresses may improvise to bring a scene to life. The playwright thus labors on the page to produce the greatest "probability of success," knowing full well that any outcome will depend on the "perilous touches" of the actors who are brought in to perform the work.[121]

---

[121] Freeman, "On the Art of Dramatic Probability," p. 175.

Lawrence's unfinished representations of both Inchbald and Lady Cahir offer a visual map of Freeman's thesis; the compositions provide some framework and scaffolding but are ultimately studies in improvisation and collaboration between the artist and the subject – and between the subject and the audience. Lawrence, like Inchbald, is interested in how the specific techniques and tools of his art can bring a scene to life, but this magic is still dependent on the creative gifts of particular performers. The subjects of Lawrence's evocative and mysterious portraits mediate and transcend his own "fit of folly," offering alternative ways to consider the legacies of the art of the actress beyond the parameters of objectification and display.

At the time of the Bentley Priory Theatricals, Inchbald was writing her memoirs, the manuscript of which she later destroyed. While we have several of her pocket diaries, these small books are masterpieces of incompleteness, full of fragments, unfinished phrases, and mysterious symbols. To engage with Inchbald and her history means embracing the realities and potential of what will always be incomplete. The powerful and lingering impression Inchbald and Lady Cahir made on Thomas Lawrence connects us to the process of their artistic production and to the aftereffects of their art. In a similar way, to wrestle more broadly with representations of actresses, female artists, and women engaged in public performance highlights many facets of the art of the actress in the eighteenth century – the celebrated, the paradoxical, and the enduring.

References

Alberge, Dalya. "Graphic Portrait of Charles II's Mistress Comes to Light." *The Guardian*, June 28, 2011, www.theguardian.com/artanddesign/2011/jun/28/nell-gwyn-charles-mistress-painting.

Albinson, A. Cassandra. "The Construction of Desire, Lawrence's Portraits of Women." In *Thomas Lawrence: Regency Power & Brilliance*, edited by A. Cassandra Albinson, Peter Funnell, and Lucy Peltz, 27–54. New Haven, CT: Yale University Press, 2011.

Albinson, A. Cassandra. "New Ambition: Experimentation and Innovation in Portraiture Practice." In *Thomas Lawrence: Regency Power & Brilliance*, edited by A. Cassandra Albinson, Peter Funnell, and Lucy Peltz, 189–216. New Haven, CT: Yale University Press, 2011.

Albinson, A. Cassandra, Peter Funnell, and Lucy Peltz, eds. *Thomas Lawrence: Regency Power & Brilliance*. New Haven, CT: Yale University Press, 2011.

Asleson, Robyn, ed. *Notorious Muse: The Actress in British Art and Culture, 1776–1812*. New Haven, CT: Yale University Press, 2003.

Asleson, Robyn, ed. *A Passion for Performance: Sarah Siddons and Her Portraitists*. Los Angeles, CA: J. Paul Getty Museum, 1999.

Baiesi, Serena. "The Influence of the Italian *Improvvisatrici* on British Romantic Women Writers: Letitia Elizabeth Landon's Response." In *British Romanticism and Italian Literature*, edited by Laura Bandiera and Diego Saglia, 181–91. Amsterdam: Rodopi, 2005.

Barchas, Janine. "Reporting on What Jane Saw 2.0: Female Celebrity and Sensationalism in Boydell's Shakespeare Gallery." *ABO: Interactive Journal for Women in the Arts, 1640–1830* 5, no. 1 (2015): 1–26.

Batchelor, Jennie, and Alison Larkin. *Jane Austen Embroidery: Regency Patterns Reimagined for Modern Stitchers*. Mineola, NY: Dover, 2020.

Baum, Kelly, Andrea Bayer, and Sheena Wagstaff, eds. *Unfinished: Thoughts Left Visible*. New York: Metropolitan Museum of Art, 2016.

Baumgärtel, Bettina, ed. *Angelica Kauffman*. Munich: Hirmer, 2020.

Berry, Mary. *The Fashionable Friends: A Comedy in Five Acts. As Performed by Their Majesties Servants at the Theatre Royale, Drury Lane*. 2nd ed. London: J. Ridgeway, 1802.

Breashears, Caroline. "Desperately Seeking Mary Anne Clarke: Scandal, Suppression, and Problems in Attribution." *Script & Print* 36, no. 1 (2012): 5–26.

Brylowe, Thora. "Angelica Kauffman and the Sister Arts." In *The Edinburgh Companion to Romanticism and the Arts*, edited by Maureen McCue and Sophie Thomas, 391–407. Edinburgh: Edinburgh University Press, 2022.

Dashkova, Ekaterina R. *The Memoirs of Princess Dashkova*. Translated and edited by Kyril Fitzlyon. Durham, NC: Duke University Press, 1995.

Davidson, Hillary. *Dress in the Age of Jane Austen: Regency Fashion*. New Haven, CT: Yale University Press, 2019.

Doran, Susan, ed. *Elizabeth and Mary: Royal Cousins, Rival Queens*. London: British Library, 2021.

Dryden, John. *Tyrannick Love, or The Royal Martyr: A Tragedy*. London: H. Herringman, 1670.

Elfenbein, Andrew. "Lesbian Aestheticism on the Eighteenth-Century Stage." *Eighteenth-Century Life* 25, no 1 (2001): 1–16.

Engel, Laura. *Austen, Actresses, and Accessories: Much Ado about Muffs*. London: Palgrave Macmillan, 2015.

Engel, Laura. *Fashioning Celebrity: Eighteenth-Century British Actresses and Strategies for Image-Making*. Columbus: Ohio State University Press, 2011.

Engel, Laura. "The Muff Affair: Fashioning Celebrity in the Portraits of Late-Eighteenth-Century British Actresses." *Fashion Theory* 13, no. 3 (2009): 279–98.

Engel, Laura. "Stage Beauties: Actresses and Celebrity Culture in the Long Eighteenth Century." *Literature Compass* 13, no. 12 (2016): 749–61.

Engel, Laura. *Women, Performance, and the Material of Memory: The Archival Tourist, 1780–1915*. London: Palgrave Macmillan, 2019.

Fraser, Flora. *The Unruly Queen: The Life of Queen Caroline*. Berkeley: University of California Press, 1997.

Freeman, Lisa A. "Mourning the 'Dignity of the Siddonian Form.'" *Eighteenth-Century Fiction* 27, nos. 3–4 (2015): 597–629.

Freeman, Lisa A. "On the Art of Dramatic Probability: Elizabeth Inchbald's *Remarks for the British Theatre*." *Theatre Survey* 62, no. 2 (2021): 163–81.

Funnell, Peter. "Lawrence among Men: Friends, Patrons and the Male Portrait." In *Thomas Lawrence: Regency Power & Brilliance*, edited by A. Cassandra Albinson, Peter Funnell, and Lucy Peltz, 1–26. New Haven, CT: Yale University Press, 2011.

Gross, Jonathan David. *The Life of Anne Damer: Portrait of a Regency Artist*. Lanham, MD: Lexington Books, 2013.

Grosvenor, Bendor. *Bright Souls: The Forgotten Story of Britain's First Female Artists*. London: Lyon & Turnbull, 2019.

Hall, Kim F. *Things of Darkness: Economies of Race and Gender in Early Modern England*. Ithaca, NY: Cornell University Press, 1995.

Hunting, Penelope. *My Dearest Heart: The Artist Mary Beale (1633–1699)*. London: Unicorn, 2019.

Hyde, Melissa, and Jennifer Milam, eds. *Women, Art, and the Politics of Identity in Eighteenth-Century Europe*. Aldershot, VT: Ashgate, 2003.

Joyce, Kristin, and Shellei Addison. *Pearls: Ornament and Obsession*. London: Thames & Hudson, 1992.

Kunz, George Frederick, and Charles Hugh Stevenson. *The Book of the Pearl: The History, Art, Science, and Industry of the Queen of Gems*. 1908. New York: Dover, 1993.

MacLeod, Catharine, and Julia Marciari Alexander, eds. *Painted Ladies: Women at the Court of Charles II*. New Haven, CT: Yale Center for British Art, 2001.

MacLeod, Catharine, and Julia Marciari Alexander. "The 'Windsor Beauties' and the Beauties Series in Restoration England." In *Politics, Transgression, and Representation at the Court of Charles II*, edited by Julia Marciari Alexander and Catharine MacLeod, 81–122. New Haven, CT: Yale Center for British Art, 2007.

Marciari Alexander, Julia, and Catharine MacLeod, eds. *Politics, Transgression, and Representation at the Court of Charles II*. New Haven: Yale Center for British Art, 2007.

McCreery, Cindy. *The Satirical Gaze: Prints of Women in Late Eighteenth-Century England*. Oxford: Clarendon, 2004.

McGirr, Elaine. "Nell Gwyn's Breasts and Colley Cibber's Shirts: Celebrity Actors and Their Famous 'Parts.'" In *Intimacy and Celebrity in Eighteenth-Century Literary Culture: Public Interiors*, edited by Emrys Jones and Victoria Joule, 13–34. London: Palgrave Macmillan, 2018.

McGirr, Elaine. "Touching Scenes: Austen, Intimacy, and Staging *Lovers' Vows*." In *Jane Austen, Sex, and Romance: Engaging with Desire in the Novels and Beyond*, edited by Nora Nachumi and Stephanie Oppenheim, 164–72. Rochester, NY: University of Rochester Press, 2022.

McPherson, Heather. *Art and Celebrity in the Age of Reynolds and Siddons*. University Park: Pennsylvania State University Press, 2017.

Mudge, Bradford. "'Enchanting *Witchery*': Sir Joshua Reynolds's *Portrait of Kitty Fisher As Cleopatra*." *Eighteenth-Century Life* 40, no. 1 (2016): 32–58.

Mudge, Bradford. "Gazing Games: Portraits and Satire in Rowlandson's *Connoisseurs*." *Eighteenth-Century Studies* 55, no. 2 (2022): 163–89.

Noble, Percy. *Anne Seymour Damer: A Woman of Art and Fashion, 1748–1828*. London: Kegan Paul, Trench, Trübner & Company, 1908.

Nussbaum, Felicity. *Rival Queens: Actresses, Performance, and the Eighteenth-Century British Theater*. Philadelphia: University of Pennsylvania Press, 2011.

Ockman, Carol, et al. *Sarah Bernhardt: The Art of High Drama*. New Haven, CT: Yale University Press, 2005.

Perry, Gill. *Spectacular Flirtations: Viewing the Actress in British Art and Theater, 1768–1820*. London: Paul Mellon Centre, 2008.

Perry, Gill, Joseph Roach, and Shearer West. *The First Actresses: Nell Gwyn to Sarah Siddons*. Ann Arbor: University of Michigan Press, 2011.

Phillips, Chelsea. *Carrying All before Her: Celebrity Pregnancy and the London Stage, 1689–1800*. Newark: University of Delaware Press, 2022.

Pointon, Marcia. *Brilliant Effects: A Cultural History of Gem Stones and Jewellery*. New Haven, CT: Yale University Press, 2009.

Porter, Linda. *Mistresses: Sex and Scandal at the Court of Charles II*. New York: Pan Macmillan, 2021.

Rauser, Amelia. *The Age of Undress: Art, Fashion, and the Classical Ideal in the 1790s*. New Haven, CT: Yale University Press, 2020.

Rauser, Amelia. *Caricature Unmasked: Irony, Authenticity, and Individualism in Eighteenth-Century English Prints*. Newark: University of Delaware Press, 2008.

Rauser, Amelia. "Living Statues and Neoclassical Dress in Late Eighteenth-Century Naples." *Art History* 38, no. 3 (2015): 462–87.

Ribeiro, Aileen. *Dress and Morality*. New York: Bloomsbury, 2003.

Roach, Joseph. *It*. Ann Arbor: University of Michigan Press, 2007.

Roman, Cynthia. "The Art of Lady Diana Beauclerk: Horace Walpole and Female Genius." In *Horace Walpole's Strawberry Hill*, edited by Michael Snodin, 155–70. New Haven, CT: Yale University Press, 2009.

Rosenfeld, Sybil. *Temples of Thespis: Some Private Theatres and Theatricals in England and Wales, 1700–1820*. London: Society for Theatre Research, 1978.

Rosenthal, Angela. *Angelica Kauffman: Art and Sensibility*. London: Paul Mellon Centre, 2006.

Rosenthal, Laura J. *Ways of the World: Theater and Cosmopolitanism in the Restoration and Beyond*. Ithaca, NY: Cornell University Press, 2020.

Roworth, Wendy Wassyng, ed. *Angelica Kauffman: A Continental Artist in Georgian England*. London: Reaktion Books, 1992.

Schmid, Susanne. "Mary Berry's *Fashionable Friends* on Stage (1801)." *The Wordsworth Circle* 43, no. 3 (2012): 172–7.

Schneider, Rebecca. *Performing Remains: Art and War in Times of Theatrical Reenactment*. London: Routledge, 2011.

Sharpe, Kevin. "'Thy Longing Country's Darling and Desire': Aesthetics, Sex, and Politics in the England of Charles II." In *Politics, Transgression, and Representation at the Court of Charles II*, edited by Julia Marciari Alexander and Catharine MacLeod, 1–32. New Haven, CT: Yale Center for British Art, 2007.

Shen, Fiona Lindsay. *Pearls: Nature's Perfect Gem*. London: Reaktion Books, 2022.

Sherriff, Mary D. "Pour l'histoire des femmes artistes: Historiographie, politique et théorie (For a History of Women Artists: Historiography, Politics, and Theory)." *Perspective* 1 (2017): 91–112.

Simon, Robin "'Strong Impressions of Their Art': Zoffany and the Theatre." In *Johan Zoffany RA: Society Observed*, edited by Martin Postle, 50–73. New Haven, CT: Yale Center for British Art, Royal Academy of Arts, 2011.

Spies-Gans, Paris A. *A Revolution on Canvas: The Rise of Women Artists in Britain and France, 1760–1830*. London: Paul Mellon Centre, 2022.

Strobel, Heidi A. *The Artistic Matronage of Queen Charlotte (1744–1818): How a Queen Promoted Both Art and Female Artists in English Society*. Lewiston, NY: Edwin Mellen, 2011.

Sunday, Skyler. "Rendering Documentary Portraiture: An Interrogation of Archival Discourse through a Critical Exploration of Nineteenth-Century Stage Actress Charlotte Cushman's Material Memory." Unpublished master's thesis, Duquesne University, 2022.

Taylor, David Francis. *The Politics of Parody: A Literary History of Caricature, 1760–1830*. New Haven, CT: Yale University Press, 2018.

Tomalin, Claire. *Mrs Jordan's Profession: The Story of a Great Actress and a Future King*. New York: Knopf, 1995.

Tuite, Clara. "Comedy, Too Fatal Emblem: Anne Damer and Occult Theatricality." *Eighteenth-Century Fiction* 27, nos. 3–4 (2015): 557–96.

Turner, Katherine. "Daphne du Maurier's *Mary Anne*: Rewriting the Regency Romance As Feminist History." *University of Toronto Quarterly* 86, no. 4 (2017): 54–77.

Vickery, Amanda. "Branding Angelica: Reputation Management in Late Eighteenth-Century England." *Journal for Eighteenth-Century Studies* 43, no. 1 (2020): 3–24.

Walpole, Horace. *Anecdotes of Painting in England*. 1786. London: Alexander Murray, 1871.

Warsh, Molly A. *American Baroque: Pearls and the Nature of Empire, 1492–1700*. Chapel Hill: University of North Carolina Press, 2018.

Webb, Richard. *Mrs D: The Life of Anne Damer (1748–1828)*. Redditch, Worcestershire: Brewin Books, 2013.

West, Shearer. *The Image of the Actor: Verbal and Visual Representation in the Age of Garrick and Kemble*. New York: St. Martin's Press, 1991.

Winn, James Anderson. *Queen Anne: Patroness of Arts*. Oxford: Oxford University Press, 2014.

Acknowledgments

I began this project before the pandemic, and it has had many twists and turns along the road to completion. I'm very grateful to Eve Tavor Bannet for her encouragement, patience, and flexibility. Much of the inspiration for *The Art of Actress* emerged from my work at the Lewis Walpole Library, Yale University, particularly my experience cocurating the exhibit *Artful Nature: Fashion and Theatricality* with the wonderful Amelia Rauser, a travel fellowship that was originally scheduled for 2020 and occurred in the summer of 2023, and most recently directing an abridged version of Mary Berry's *Fashionable Friends* at the Library in May 2023. Special thanks to Cindy Roman, Susan Walker, Nicole Bouche, and the Lewis Walpole Library staff. Also, to the incomparable Joseph Roach, who championed this project from the beginning.

I am truly indebted to my dear colleagues and friends involved in the Pittsburgh Gender Scholars writing group, with extra special thanks to Jessie Ramey, Kathleen Newman, Linda Kinnahan, Faith Barrett, Catherine Evans, Kipp Dawson, and Emily Rutter. Grateful thanks as well to the members of the 18th-Century Zoom Bistro, Kristina Straub, Marilyn Francus, Teri Doerksen, and Nora Nachumi for support, love, and sanity. I continue to be enriched and inspired by my colleagues in eighteenth-century studies, with special thanks to Elaine McGirr, Marlis Schweitzer, Diana Solomon, Jean Marsden, Heather McPherson, Jennie Batchelor, Chloe Wigston Smith, Heidi Strobel, Jennifer Germann, Carolyn Day, Caroline Gonda, Ellen Malenas Ledoux, Susan Carlile, Norbert Schurer, Greg Clingham, Tanya Caldwell, Leslie Ritchie, Heather Ladd, Jess Banner, Bradford Mudge, David Francis Taylor, Ros Ballaster, Chelsea Phillips, and Laura Rosenthal.

I am grateful for my students, who continue to inspire my fascination with actress studies, particularly the members of my recent seminars "Women in Nineteenth-Century Theater" and "Fashion and the Body on Film and Stage." Thanks to my English department chair, Danielle St. Hilaire, and the Duquesne University Office of Research for awarding me a Presidential Writing Grant to work on this project. Grateful thanks to Mike Begnal for his outstanding copyediting. Finally, incalculable gratitude goes to my fantastic family for listening to me natter on about eighteenth-century actresses and paintings for all these years.

9 781108 977906